YOUR HAND

YOUR HAND

SIMPLE PALMISTRY
FOR EVERYONE

BETTINA LUXON AND
JILL GOOLDEN

HARMONY BOOKS/NEW YORK

Published in the United States in 1984 by Harmony Books, a division of Crown Publishers, Inc., One Park Avenue, New York, New York 10016, and simultaneously in Canada by General Publishing Company Limited

Published in Great Britain in 1983 by William Heinemann, 10 Upper Grosvenor Street, London W1K 9DA

HARMONY and colophon are trademarks of Crown Publishers, Inc.

Manufactured in Great Britain

Library of Congress Cataloging in Publication Data

Luxon, Bettina.
    Your hand: simple palmistry for everyone.
    1. Palmistry.   I. Goolden, Jill.   II. Title.
BF921.L88   1984   133.6   84-3763
ISBN 0–517–55502–6 (pbk.)

10 9 8 7 6 5 4 3 2 1

First American Edition

CONTENTS

For Betty Reyburn,
with our thanks

The quote from *Mind Map* by Anthony Masters
is by kind permission of Methuen, London.

I

INTRODUCTION

On the face of it, palmistry seems to be pretty far removed from everyday life. For some obscure reason, people putting this ancient science to use invariably surround themselves with mystery. Shrouded with sinister fringed scarves, cluttered up with all the inexplicable paraphernalia of the occult (ouija boards and crystal balls *et al*) they frankly frighten off most reasonable human beings.

No one feels safe with the unknown, and unfortunately palmistry has been allowed to slip into the fringes of magic. But we are here to bring it out into the light again and to tell you that palmistry has absolutely nothing to do with boards and balls and has no recognizable link with magic and mystery. It is simply a useful and practical device which can be learnt.

To become a proficient palmist, you do not have to possess unnatural powers. This ancient art is available to anyone capable of following a very simple set of rules. Forget the scarves, the middle European names, the mumbo jumbo of the seaside pier. And rethink the whole concept of palmistry.

It is a bit like a recipe. Take the ingredients, follow the method, and even a novice can work out how to bake a passable cake. At the first attempt, the cake may not be perfect in every respect; but with a little practice the cook will be able to bake any number of cakes without even glancing at the recipe, almost intuitively.

So it is with palmistry. From the shape of the hand, the proportions of the fingers, the pattern of the lines on the palm, definite character traits can be read with, some would say uncanny, accuracy. But palmistry is not uncanny. It is based on practical fortune telling, passed down through the ages and all the way round the globe. Ever since the discovery of finger prints and the realization that each individual has unique palms, hands have been considered in some way or other as the outward and visible sign of the inner person.

And this is not such an illogical notion as it may appear. For not only are our hands the principal ambassadors of our bodies (they are, after all, the most important carrier of physical feelings to the brain – you would always, for instance, feel your way in the dark with your hands); palms are also, according to scholars from the ancient world to the present day, ambassadors of our subconscious as well. Writing earlier this century, for instance, Dr Charlotte Wolff, a psychologist who used hand analysis extensively in her work, called the hand 'the visible part of the brain', and just as each brain is original, so too, is each hand.

Back in the days when witches were being burnt at the stake, on through the time when palm-reading gypsies were expelled from the land, to the present day of hand analysis and research, it has been believed that hands could be used to catch a glimpse of the inner soul.

It is now acknowledged that when we are born, the major part of our character is already formed. And if you look at a new-born baby's hands, you will see that the principal lines on the palm are clearly defined as well. The minor lines, too, could start to show at this stage, although the majority of fine lines develop with age.

The principal lines – the Life line, the Head line and the Heart line – considered both individually, and read together – shed light on their owner's character and on some major events. In themselves, these lines are likely to remain unaltered for life, although their meaning can occasionally be changed by the appearance of auxiliary signs.

The minor lines not only throw more light on personality, but also highlight talents and drawbacks, achievements and short-comings as well. Considering all the lines, not only individually, but related to each other and to the hand shape as well, the hand can, with the benefit of experience (and the help of this book) literally be read.

Working through chapter by chapter, you will not only be able to interpret other people's hands, but your own as well. It will be possible to tell how your career is likely to develop; whether you are a 'sticker' who will make a success of your job, or a bit of a dreamer who will find fulfilment in other ways. You will be able to tell if your material and financial position will alter, or stay the same; you can plot the path of your passions and see the likely course of romances and affairs.

Once the techniques are mastered, there will be few characters you will be unable to crack, few areas of a person's life which will remain concealed from view, since it is possible to gain insight into emotions and intellect and to see the motive force behind each individual's behaviour.

Studying the palms of the hands carefully, the reader is able to see what sort of a start the subject had in life, and to assess the strongest influences of character. Moving towards the present day, significant events can be isolated, and the course of life prior to the reading identified. Moving on to the future, however, only possibilities present themselves.

While character is fairly fixed, we all have to believe that events can be altered by our own free will. Once you have become quite accomplished as a palmist, and feel confident about predicting the future, it is important to understand that you see only what will happen if the subject continues on the current course. Opportunities present themselves, and depending upon other people, other circumstances, and upon the subject's innate character and frame of mind at the time, they may either be taken up or ignored.

It would be very discouraging, and we think wrong, to believe that our lives are predestined from birth; that we ourselves have no influence over our own fates. If something unpleasant looms on the horizon and we foresee it in time, we fortunately have the ability to alter course. So if an event presents itself in the hand, it is by no means a foregone conclusion that it will happen. The opportunity will be recognized by the subject, certainly, but could well never be taken up, and in time, not only the opportunity, but also the linked pattern in the hand will disappear.

The fine lines in the hand change shape constantly, so hand reading need not be a one-off affair. Anyone's hands, including your own, of course, will be seen to alter very slightly from month to month. If you study the same pair of hands fairly frequently, the added concentration needed to perceive the change, and to interpret the subtle shift of lines could well sharpen your own powers of intuition.

It seems highly likely that we are all born with a sixth sense, but few of us give this valuable asset much chance to develop. When you begin to concentrate deeply on the pattern of a subject's life, you could well find that for the duration of the reading your minds seem to be in tune . . . Certainly it is perfectly possible to read a palm like a book, but it is also possible to add your own valuable intuitive interpretation as well.

READING HANDS

Your Hand has been designed like a succinct encyclopaedia of life. You can dip into it like a dictionary, to find the meaning of a particular line; or pick a character trait at random, and find its related pattern in the hand. Without more ado, you can get a pretty good idea of a person's character just by working through the book matching illustration with hand.

At first it is not essential to memorize the meaning of every shape, every pattern, every line. The book can be kept to hand as a guide, and used as simply as any reference book. But if, however, you want to take the useful device of palmistry just one step further, so that your readings become more spontaneous and more precise, it pays to follow the method suggested here and, in time, to memorize as much as you can.

Learning about palmistry is all to do with experience. By reading as many hands as possible (and, if you like, studying hand prints as well), you will gradually feel quite at home with the shapes, the textures, the lines, and interpretation will become much less book-bound and more intuitive and natural.

Whichever way you choose to approach the business of palmistry however, either superficially or more seriously, there are a few essentials to grasp, which put you on the first step towards reading hands. For a start, you must acquaint yourself with the names of all the different features of the hand.

These traditionally have an astrological bias. From the very earliest writings on palmistry that have survived, it appears that in ancient times, the hand was considered as a mini-horoscope. In time, palmistry earned an individual status of its own and the astrological link was severed, but the names were already well established, and so have remained.

We have, wherever logical, stuck to the accepted names, so as to break with the traditions of palmistry as little as possible and maintain the ancient links. However, in certain instances where the more recent latinate names (ascribed to various hand shapes, for instance) have seemed to be misleading, we have substituted more straightforward terms of our own: the 'psychic' hand, for instance, has been renamed the Oval hand; 'philosophic' hand, the Knotty hand, in the interests of easier identification.

All the different hand shapes are described in detail and illustrated in Chapter 3. So here, we will concentrate on the map of the hand itself, identifying the fingers, the mounts on the palms, and the lines, seen, of course, palm side up.

On the following two pages are 'maps' to help you identify the fingers, mounts, principal and minor lines. The three lines shown in the illustration on the left can alter from hand to hand in length and, to an extent, in direction and position; however, all palms hold them in some shape or form. Each finger and mount is dealt with individually in Chapter 4, but more importantly they are used as identification for direction of lines: for instance, a branch from the Life line would have a very different meaning of it made for the mount of Saturn than if it made for the mount of Jupiter. It is therefore useful if these names can be memorized as early as possible, but you will soon find yourself naturally referring to them by their correct names as you begin to practise.

Next, we move on to the minor lines of Destiny, the Sun, Affection, Marriage, Children, Travel and the Girdle of Venus. By no means will all these lines necessarily appear in every hand. Sometimes one or other, or even several, will be absent altogether, or will show up in a slightly modified form. In Chapter 6 the meanings of all lines and forms are analysed, but at this stage, let us reassure you that you are not peculiar if you cannot find any one of these minor lines in your hand.

Also identified on this map are two important incidental signs which will be dealt with in detail later, but which are often referred to in relation to other lines.

You will notice that the left and right palms are never exactly alike. And indeed, in palmistry, each is attributed with a different significance. The left hand reveals the characteristics with which the subject was born, and the right, how these are put to use. When you become proficient enough to read not just a character, but also events, the left hand will reveal what has happened in the past, and the right, what is still to come.

Fingers, Mounts and Principal Lines

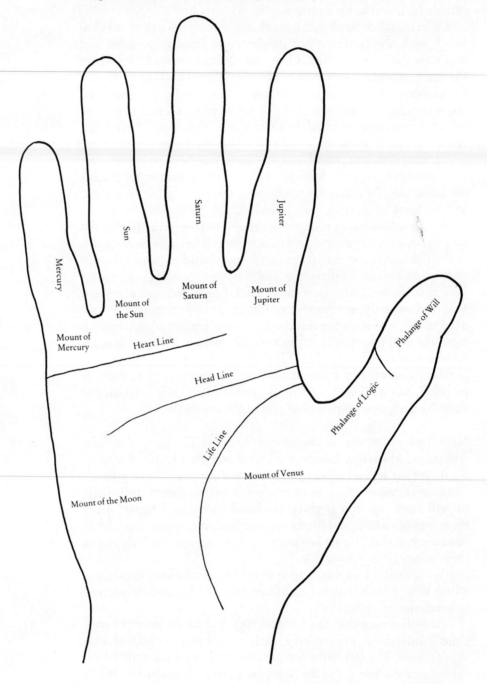

Mercury

Sun

Saturn

Jupiter

Mount of
Saturn

Mount of
Jupiter

Mount of
the Sun

Phalange of Will

Mount of
Mercury

Heart Line

Phalange of Logic

Head Line

Phalange of Logic

Life Line

Mount of Venus

Mount of the Moon

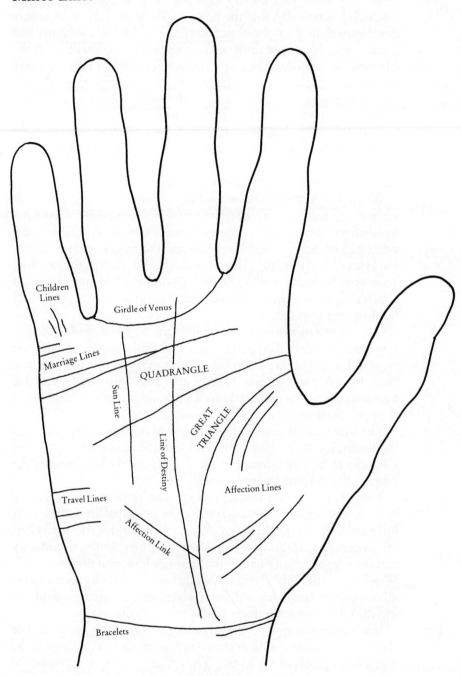

Children
Lines

Girdle of Venus

Marriage Lines

QUADRANGLE

Sun Line

GREAT
TRIANGLE

Line of Destiny

Travel Lines

Affection Lines

Affection Link

Bracelets

All this is not as arbitrary as it may at first appear. Scientific research has revealed that the left side of the brain is more highly developed than the right. Since each side of the body is controlled by the opposite side of the brain, the right hand (controlled by the left hemisphere of the brain) will therefore reflect more activity and be more topical than the left hand (controlled by the less active right hemisphere of the brain) which will remain much more static, showing fewer changes from birth.

With left handed people who have opted to favour the left hand instead of the right, the rules are reversed; the right hand then shows the innate characteristics, and in time, the past; leaving the left hand to reveal development and point to the future.

When you first embark on reading someone's hands, you must warn them that it could take quite a time, and to save their arms and hands from getting tired, it helps to rest them on a cushion, palm side up. The hands should be open and the fingers stretched out, but relaxed and not taut. Throughout the duration of the reading, your concentration will be helped if you keep contact with your subject's hands, either resting the fingers on your own, or gently holding on to the finger tips.

It is not essential to read the hand from the wrist, and so long as you can reverse our illustrations in your mind, you can sit opposite your subject, reading from the fingers instead. We suggest you tactfully ask your subject to save any questions until you have finished, since constant interruptions could destroy your chain of thought. So here goes:

The first thing to do is to feel the give in the finger tips, and then the flexibility of the palm, (these are dealt with at the beginning of Chapter 3), before moving on to identifying the hand shape, the fingers, the mounts and the thumbs.

Your Hand is written in exactly the sequence you should follow, moving from hand shapes, to the principal lines, the minor lines and then the incidental marks. Each line and mark, with all its idiosyncrasies, should be considered in turn, both individually and, as suggested, in relation to the other lines and marks as well. Slowly a picture will emerge, first rather disjointedly, but in time all the component parts will interrelate and gel together, explaining the whys and wherefores of the subject's life.

If as a complete novice, hand reading becomes too protracted an affair for your long-suffering subject to tolerate, you can instead work from prints of the hands. These can be made in a number of ways, the simplest of which is on a photocopier.

Placing the hands palm down where you would usually put the paper on the machine, either both together if there is room or else one at a time, it is possible to get a very detailed impression of the hand, including even the fine lines. Sometimes for this rather unusual adaptation of the photocopying machine (none of the makes we know actually had palms in mind when they finalized their design) it is necessary to make a few experiments with the light-dark switch before you achieve a good picture of the palms. Since, when photographed in this way, the images are reversed, it is a good plan to write 'Right' and 'Left' on each hand to remind you which is which.

If you do not have access to a good copier, and want to make a very professional job of your prints, you can make them in ink, with lino print. The equipment you need is a rubber roller about 5ins wide, a tube of water-based lino printing ink, a sheet of glass, a thin piece of foam or rubber and good quality cartridge paper.

First squeeze about two inches of ink on to the middle of the glass, and then roll repeatedly over the ink with your roller, until it is evenly covered with a thin coat. Place a sheet of paper on top of the sheet of rubber, roll the roller back and forth over the palm and the fingers of the hand to be printed, and then press the ink-covered hand firmly down on to the sheet of paper. The reason for the sheet of foam or rubber underneath the paper is to provide a little softness to a hard surface and so allow all parts of the hand, even the slightly hollow centre of the palm, to make an impression. Press down hard on the back of the hand for good measure then lift off gently from the wrist, while holding the paper down to prevent smudging.

You should have before you a very clear print; if not, try again, possibly sliding both rubber and paper over the edge of the table, to be able to exert extra pressure on the centre of the hand. When you have finished, the ink (you will be relieved to hear) washes off the hand quite easily, but remains fast in the print.

An easier, cheaper method of making prints at home is to use an old tube of lipstick instead of the ink. Rub the lipstick evenly all over the inside of the hand, smoothing out any lumps. Then make the print in exactly the same way, substituting, if you wish, a folded tea towel for the foam rubber. Again, the lipstick will wash easily off the hands, but will need to be fixed on the paper, being apt to smudge. A quick squirt of hair lacquer will achieve this adequately, but for further protection of any prints while you are poring over them, you can cover the paper with a layer of wrinkle-free cling film. Taking prints with either of these methods also reverses the image, so again identify each print with 'Left' or 'Right' as soon as it is made.

Studying prints is exactly the same as studying the actual hands, except that you lose some of the personal contact, of course. Usually it is possible either with an actual hand, or with an inanimate facsimile to see all that you need to see with the naked eye. But a good magnifying glass will reveal more detail, if needs be. However, as a novice, you could find the additional material shown up by the magnifying glass more a hindrance than a help, since to start with we recommend that you concentrate on the principal and minor lines, considering the fine lines only if they constitute a recognizable mark (a cross, for instance, or a square).

If you make hand prints, it is a good idea to keep them, not only as a reference of the hands you have read, but also as a reminder of all the particular features you have identified. Looking back over hands you have already studied is one of the easiest ways to familiarize yourself with all the theory, and to lift palmistry from two-dimensional illustrations into a practical device that works; an art which comes to life.

Having read the method, you are now ready to think of the basic ingredients, which are contained in the following five chapters. We suggest you skim through these first on your own, before putting them into practice on an actual hand.

Beyond the ingredients, we have devised some recipes which relate to partners and careers. These you can use either as an extension of your hand-reading analysis, or just on their own, for fun. If you choose to use this book simply for dipping into from time to time, the index at the end of the book will be your best ally, acting as an instant guide to particular interests or characteristics.

One last point we must make before launching you into your first reading, concerns time. In the past, we believe in the interests of sensation, some palmists have claimed that a precise time can be put on past and future events. We do not agree. As a microcosm of our lives, the palm is too small to be that precise. The best that you can do is to generalize, judging roughly where an influence affects a line, whether it be at the beginning, in the middle or near the end, in the twilight years. Sometimes it is impossible to put a time on a prediction or on something that has happened in the past, but if it shows up clearly in the hand, you can assume that the event is not that far away.

3

HAND TYPES

The brief definition of 'palmist' in *Chambers Twentieth Century Dictionary* is 'one who tells fortune from the lines on the palm'. So economical is this description that it leaves out a major part of this complex science. Certainly the lines go far to explain character, talents and nature as well as past and future events, but a much broader outline of a person's make-up can be deduced simply by the shape, proportions and texture of the hand itself.

Just as hands can be qualified by type, so too can their owners. The link between one sort of hand, for instance, and a down-to-earth, no nonsense nature is pretty well assured. And so before getting out the magnifying glass and scrutinizing every last line, every mark and every pattern, it is worth spending a little time contemplating the hand as a whole.

Hands are as good an outward and visible sign of the inner being as any we have. For centuries, philosophers have believed that there is a link between the inner psyche and the outer manifestation of self. Of course not everyone is true to himself in his behaviour; but we could work on the assumption that everyone is true to himself at least in his hands.

Earlier this century, one or two renowned palmists committed their art to books, and claimed cheirognomy – the analysis of the shape of the hands and fingers – 'denotes the breeding, racial and more general characteristics'.* We are much more conscious now of a meritocracy and are not going to be fobbed off with the notion that class distinction is actually *visible*. To deduce race from hand shapes seems a little pointless, as well, since, apart from obvious

*Cheiro's *You and Your Hand*, Sphere Books, 1974

colour differences, hand shapes are the same throughout the world. So definitely 'general characteristics' now predominate.

But before we proceed to try to solve the riddle of which characteristics belong to which hands, there are a few more fallacies and old wives' tales to dismiss. Down through the ages various banal observations have erroneously been linked with palmistry. Hard and unsupple skin in women, for instance, has been associated with lack of privilege and the need – or delight – in hard manual work. This skin type is no more a social indicator than it is the result of the wrong detergent (as advertisements would have us believe). It has its own explanation, and is linked to a particular character trait instead. Likewise in men, coarse, square hands have tended to be lumped into the 'manual worker' category. Certainly hard, physical jobs demand a certain degree of strength, and would be quite unsuitable for men with either feeble frames or delicate hands but it is quite wrong to attribute all hard, square hands to artisans.

One of the most telling superficial features of the hand is the 'give' in the centre of the palm. Quite distinct from skin texture, the elasticity of the palm itself is one of the first personality indicators you should use. To do the 'palm test', first take either of your subject's hands in your own. With your thumb in the centre of the palm, and your fingers stretched out across the back of the hand, press to feel the extent of give between fingers and thumb.

Sometimes you will find that the hand is hard, with little elasticity. This hand undoubtedly belongs to a hard worker, who fully throws himself into the job in hand, ignoring any opportunities for shirking responsibilities. This is the sort of person who is prepared to work around the clock, a great achiever, but neither through being pushy, nor through using guile. Among the less appealing features of such a personality is the ease with which he or she can be whipped into a rage or temper. Inclined to be self opinionated – and a bit of a loner – the hard-handed individual tends to fly off the handle immediately he fails to get his own way.

Less usual is the exceptionally hard hand, feeling almost as though it is solid the whole way through. This type of hand reflects a very stubborn character, who is usually rather difficult to get on with. Timid and withdrawn, such people are natural introverts who retain the ability to cut themselves off totally from the outside world, sometimes receding into their shells for several days at a time. Not surprisingly, they make friends with difficulty, not least because they prefer their own company to that of others.

The most common texture of hand is soft and springy. People with this characteristic are the born survivors, who can cope, no matter what is thrown in front of them. Tending to be assertive types, the go-getters of the world, the holders of elastic palms rise early, and face the day and whatever it brings with enthusiasm from then on. They are easy people to get on with in the main, but they can be a little ruthless if something they consider to matter a lot is at stake.

Exceptionally soft hands, with very fine skin texture, rather like babies' hands to touch, are usually the most attractive to look at and, coincidentally, belong to the aesthetes among us. These types take a great pride in their own appearance, and in their surroundings. Loving nothing better than to show off, they are very kind and generous hosts. Their homes will be comfortable and immaculate – although the credit for the latter feature invariably goes to someone else . . . for soft, pliable hands almost always point to a lazy nature. Born hedonists, these people would rather see someone else do the work, while they enjoy themselves to the full. Their 'can't be bothered' attitude can even be felt in their hand shake, which tends to be weak and limp.

Having discovered all that you can from the texture of the hand, it is time to consider its shape. Begin by comparing as many different hands as possible in order to get an idea of the variety of shapes and proportions. No two hands are exactly alike, but there are essentially five basic shapes: square, spatulate, oval, oblique and knotty, and each can give you a rough guide to a person's character, which will reveal itself in more detail when you come to study the lines.

We will take the reasonably common **square** hand type first. The most significant feature of the square hand is that it does not taper either in the palm or the fingers, the sides of each – or indeed all – being parallel. The only line which does not agree with the over-all square shape is the dividing line at the top of the palm where the fingers begin. In most hands of any shape, this line tends to curve downwards beneath the fingers of the Sun and Mercury, which denotes that any wealth or possessions owned by the subject have been worked for strenuously. When this line cuts across without dipping down, i.e. running parallel to the wrist, you can assume that the subject has had a very easy life from the start.

Square hands fall into two distinct classes, those with short fingers, and those with long. Short-fingered customers tend to be very straightforward and down to earth. Seeing is believing; you would find it very difficult to convince people with this shape of hand of the existence of the supernatural, for instance, they believe in themselves, and little else beyond that. The element of fate plays a very small part in their lives, and so, as you might expect, you seldom find a line of Destiny in this shape of hand.

The Square Hand

Indeed, it is unusual in square hands with short, square fingers to find many lines at all. Usually the subject's straightforward approach to life is reflected in the existence only of a Life line, Head line and Heart line. Imagination is seldom a strong point – except, curiously enough, in the kitchen; this shape of hand is found in chefs and good cooks too frequently to be merely co-incidental.

Square-handed, short-fingered types find it difficult to concentrate for long. They often have big ideas, and may well embark on major projects, but seldom finish the job, since either distraction or boredom sets in first. If this type of hand is particularly small, you will find its owner to be lacking in any sort of ambition; the projects won't even be taken on in the first instance . . .

Square hands with long, square fingers tell a rather different tale. These belong to all the great achievers among us; those who not only take on quite considerable tasks, but also get them done. Very capable people usually have this hand type; those who you can rely upon not to let you down. Very hard workers; if they are up to the job in the first place, you can be sure that they will shortly be on top of it. If this hand shape is combined with a strong, long Head line, its owner will be a born leader, and could well make headway either in politics, or high in the hierarchy of the armed services.

The Spatulate Hand

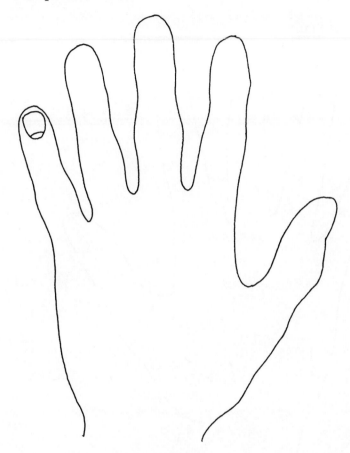

Spatulate hands are not, it must be said, the most attractive to look at, but aspiring palmists should certainly not be put off by appearances. These hands have wedge shaped, flat finger tips, the nails splaying out to be wider at the top than at the cuticle. The fingers are waisted above the main knuckle, the thumbs are waisted, and the palms are bulbous below a slight waist where the fingers join the palm. And contrary to appearances, they belong to artistic, creative characters with a real flair for aesthetics; those with a good eye for colour, for design and detail. Many gifted artists and sculptors have this type of hand, as do draughtsmen and architects. The hand shape itself may appear to be clumsy, but is in fact far from it, since it is so frequently found in professions and careers which demand fine work and great attention to detail. People with spatulate hands are generally very humanitarian. They are extremely aware of the people around them and are usually kind, considerate and generous.

The Oval Hand

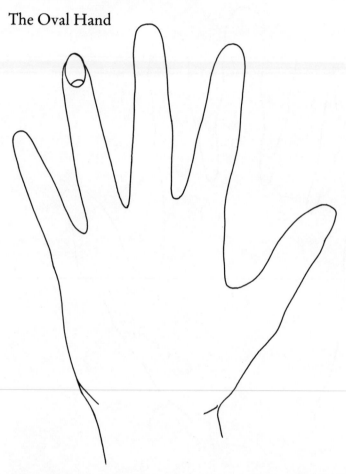

Oval shaped hands are undoubtedly the most pleasing to look at. The palm is roughly egg-shaped, ending at the wrist with a sweeping curve. The fingers are slender and gently rounded at the tips, with perfectly regular oval nails. Nine times out of ten, this hand type belongs to a woman, and will be found in association with very fine skin texture, a soft palm and very faintly marked lines. The (female) owners of these hands are very sensuous. They act like magnets to men, and certainly make the most of any masculine advances, responding with great feminine charm. If they fall in love for real, it will be for keeps, and they will remain loyal to their man for ever, despite any temptation to stray, or provocation to go. They are rather self-indulgent, loving beauty and endeavouring to be surrounded by beautiful things.

Generous and warm natured, oval-handed types choose their friends and colleagues very wisely because they are instinctively very good character judges. The oval hand has in the past sometimes been called the psychic hand, presumably because of the unusual powers of intuition associated with this shape.

The less enviable characteristics, balancing out these very good points, are a tendency to be self-centred and opinionated. Never shy, those with oval hands can be self-obsessed. But they have little will-power, and can be easily led, regularly falling under the influence of others.

The same skin texture is occasionally found in men, who could well have, in a modified form, some of these traits. They are likely to interact extremely well with women on all levels (including in bed), be warm, kind-hearted and generous. However, they too can tend to be rather weak-willed and easily led. When judging any skin texture, incidentally, be sure that 'soft' does not simply mean well cared for, as in the case of doctors and dentists. The continued protection of hand cream and gloves can, in fact, disguise a harder hand texture underneath.

The Oblique Hand

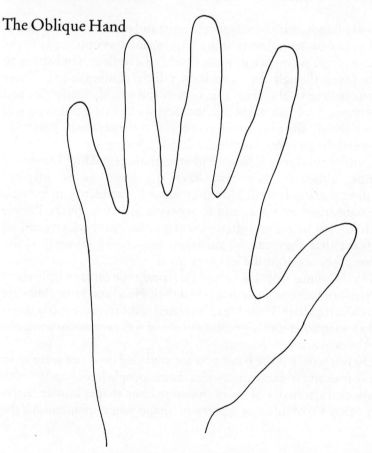

The **oblique** hand has a long, long palm and long fingers, usually an average length thumb. The fingers all incline towards the finger of the Sun. The skin texture is generally fairly soft, with a tendency to be clammy. The leaning of the fingers is read as a weak sign, the loose meaning being that if things are not entirely sunny, the subject finds it difficult to cope. Very indecisive, this person can easily be bossed about, will never make a leader, and would be well advised not to set up a business venture on his own.

In a relationship, the holder of the oblique hand will almost certainly be the underdog, not reluctantly but quite happily so, since the main life objective seems to be 'anything for a quiet life'. Shying away from responsibility, the struggle for achievement is certainly not a natural part of such a subject's make up. But these people are very methodical and meticulous in what they do. They tend to operate slowly, but none the less get good results.

They are kind and considerate, although such thoughtful gestures as remembering a birthday, for instance, may well be missed, because they find it difficult – or distasteful – to think ahead. A final generalization on the oblique hand is that very often this is a sign that the person was, and perhaps still is, very dependent on his or her mother.

Knotty hands, with pronounced joints and definite 'waists' above and below the main joints of the fingers, and less noticeably in the centre of the palm, are in most cases, an excellent hand shape to have (even though they can look a little cumbersome). These hands belong to the great thinkers of the world, academics and inventors. From an early age, possessors of this hand type will shoot ahead, showing great powers of concentration, perseverance and the patience for minute detail.

Usually such people have vivid imaginations and highly original minds, although they also have the logic to be inspired mathematicians as well. However, there is a tendency to become over-absorbed in work, and to worry a little too much. People with knotty hands are often absent-minded-professor types, so brilliant that they can be mistaken for cranks. Slightly chilly lovers, they are none the less very loyal.

On the minus side, owners of this hand type can be a little short on sense of humour – particularly if their Head and Heart lines are too close together. If the Head line itself is short, regrettably this is rather an unfortunate sign, since nothing will ever really work out for the possessor of this sign.

Do not worry if the hand you are studying does not seem to fit easily into any of these categories. Some people have hands which show characteristics of more than one basic shape: knotty hands can often be oblique or square in shape while maintaining the

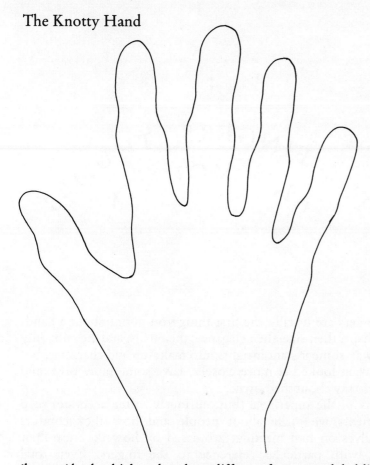

'knotty' look which makes them different from a model oblique or square hand. There are also hands, usually with square palms, with fingers of several different types. In these cases, consider the dominant shape of the hand but bear in mind as well the influences of the other hand types represented in a 'mixed' hand.

4

THE FINGERS, THUMBS AND MOUNTS

The fingers are usually the first thing you notice about a hand: their shape, their size, their elegance, their nails, and they not only give away some instant insights into make-up and character, but also, when looked at more closely, have some more profound things to say about their owner.

Many of the superficial (but, curiously, often accurate) snap judgements we make about people and how they conduct themselves on first meeting, are based on how they use their hands, with particular reference to the fingers. Even total strangers unwittingly let us see a little of themselves through their hands. You can tell a bit about the person sitting opposite you in a bus, for instance, if he or she appears to be absent-mindedly counting the fingers of one hand, or holding both thumbs firmly in fists. The soft handshake with little pressure from the fingers is the weak man's or woman's own ambassador, while finger strumming quickly exposes anyone with a highly-strung temperament.

Some of the most obvious signs have already assumed a place among well-known superstitions, and so are easily dismissed as the prattlings of old wives . . . However, they have solid foundation, and even though they have been passed down to us as folklore, should not be believed less than if they had been discovered by eminent scientists today. The old adage that 'money slips through your fingers' is accurate because large gaps between the fingers mean extravagance and an inability to save. The two were obviously linked in legend, and centuries on, the statement is used only metaphorically.

Fingers clamped tightly together imply a very secretive nature. This person gives little away, and in acute cases can be rather introverted and withdrawn. While walking along, you will notice that some people hold on tightly to their thumbs, clenching them inside a tight fist. This tendency could well have given rise to the expression 'tight fisted' since it is nearly always a sign of meanness, selfishness and closeness with money. To give people who hold their thumbs their due, however, they are frequently nervous, tense types and their apparent parsimony could well just be an extension of their general caution.

There are several rather obvious, incidental signs of nerves. The cracking of knuckles, for instance, is a giveaway that someone is very highly strung. Nail-biting, too, another disfiguring habit, is a sign of tension and worry, and almost invariably, nibblers are rather jumpy and irritable, tending to make snap decisions and to act irrationally and impulsively.

Finger strumming is often read as a sign of boredom, but this is not so. Tension, again, is frequently the cause. When the mind is somewhere else, worrying away about this and that, finger drumming is the outward sign. All these indications are usually obvious, even to the layman, but there are others which, once learnt, become equally obvious.

If you look at the back of the hand, where the fingers begin, you will see that the line of their departure is either level, or sloping down towards the finger of Mercury. In other words, the knuckles on the back of the hand either form a straight line parallel to the wrist, or slope down towards the outside of the hand. The straight line indicates a good start and an easy life, whereas the slope denotes struggles. The more accentuated the slope, the more difficult the path to success.

The flexibility of the fingers has a direct parallel with the flexibility of outlook and way of life. If the fingers and thumbs are quite pliable, so too will be their owner's whole attitude. The person with flexible fingers is a happy-go-lucky sort, and approaches all events and eventualities with an open mind. If the fingers are too flexible, however, capable of bending right back on themselves, it shows that their owner is altogether too carefree and irresponsible, tending just to sit back and allow others to take the load.

Stiff fingers, by contrast, with very little give, belong to those who tend to be very set in their ways. Narrow-minded and reactionary, these are the unbending types who will never change their minds.

You do not have to get very close to someone to notice whether their fingers all sweep up at the tips, and this is an indication that they are potentially psychic. Deeply absorbed in people – and, it must be said, in gossip – they drink up information and, having pondered on it for a while, add a unique insight of their own. They tend to have a fast-working brain, occasionally too fast for their own good, because it is able to jump ahead of events.

As you will have deduced, you can tell quite a bit about a person before you even sit down to study the sundry features and traits in detail. When you are giving a reading, although the fingers are not of paramount importance, they certainly deserve independent study of their own, individually and in relation to each other.

The pads of the finger tips, for example, can tell you about willpower. Taking each finger in turn between your Jupiter finger and thumb, squeeze the cushion behind the nail to discover if it is soft or firm. Soft finger-print pads imply that a person is easily dominated and easily led. Very soft hearted, these are the easiest people to order around. Firm cushions, on the other hand, belong to those who are more self willed. Having strong feelings about doing things their own way, these people intensely dislike being told what to do, and do not take kindly either to criticism or advice.

The length of the fingers in relationship to the length of the palm, reveals further information. Comparatively long fingers (almost as long as the palm, that is) belong to people who are generally gregarious and popular. They are neither greedy nor envious, but more often than not, things tend to go their way.

Very long fingers, as long as, or even longer than the palm, denote a greater interest in the mental aspects of life than the physical. Concerned with idealism and ideas, these people put the basic human urges such as sex and gluttony pretty low on their list of priorities.

Short fingers, on the other hand, imply a lusty sex drive. These belong to less complicated types, who have little time for refinement and detail. People with much shorter fingers than palms can be relied upon to aim high, but they do not necessarily have the wherewithal to realize their plans. This is especially true if the fingers are very short indeed, since this, combined with a short thumb and short Head line, denotes lack of intellect. Short fingers with very tiny, flat nails in conjunction with a Simian Line (see page 44) are, incidentally, one of the signs of mongolism.

To read each finger in relation to all the others, first it is necessary to set an average. It is no use trying to judge if a Jupiter finger, for instance is long or short, unless we first decide on the norm. Usually finger lengths are judged in relation to the Saturn finger, and the illustration here shows average comparative lengths. In few hands, however, will you find all fingers in both hands to be average; usually an unusual feature will be apparent, and so here we describe the meanings of some of the commoner traits.

Taking **Jupiter** first, if this, the index finger, is very long – almost as long as Saturn – it shows a person with a very strong will. With plenty of self-confidence, drive and ambition, this character will push on in life maybe at the cost of others. If the finger naturally sits slightly in front of the others it reveals great powers of leadership.

A short Jupiter finger, on the other hand, is often linked with an inferiority complex. Lacking in drive, holders of this feature find it difficult to make headway, and because of their shortcomings, have a tendency towards jealousy and envy. If the finger naturally hangs back behind the others, it shows a reluctance to take on any responsibilities.

Crooked fingers (unless caused by an accident) are never a good sign. If the Jupiter finger is permanently bent, it is a sign of untrustworthiness.

Since **Saturn** is the finger by which all the others are judged, it is difficult to assess its length comparatively. Sometimes, however, rather than the adjacent fingers appearing long, the Saturn finger itself definitely seems to be short, and in this instance its meaning is impulsiveness. Tending to rush into things without giving due thought, holders of this characteristic are easily influenced and can frequently be led astray by strong-minded friends.

Where the finger tips are concerned, Saturn is most likely of all to be the odd finger out, and its deviating shape is another pointer towards character. If it appears to be unusually pointed, it shows an easy-going nature, and indicates the kind of character who will put off doing today what can be shelved until tomorrow.

A square-tipped Saturn finger, on the other hand, belongs to a deep thinker, who will never act impulsively without careful consideration.

A crooked finger of Saturn points to an over-morbid outlook and reveals a side of someone's nature which is difficult to please. If the finger instead of being crooked, is twisted, the implication is that this person has a tendency to be cruel.

The **Sun** finger has very pleasant associations. If it is long – noticeably longer than the Jupiter finger – and the mount beneath it is firm, it reveals a very loveable nature. This is also accentuated by springy finger tips. Holders of long, straight Sun fingers tend to be the gentle types with a fondness for children and animals. If this finger tends to be favoured – used prominently instead of the Jupiter finger, that is – it shows artistic tendencies, particularly in the literary field.

Too long a Sun finger, however, reaching up to join Saturn, shows a love of gambling, and points to the person who may well take too many chances in life.

The short Sun finger reveals unfortunate impetuosity, and its owner will often act without thinking and be prone to make mistakes. This is a sign of the muddled thinker who is unable to make – or act on – a plan.

When the Sun finger in either hand is crooked, the signs are that this person will encounter many drawbacks in life. Achievements will be hard to come by, if they can ever be reached at all. Money tends to be the idol of holders of this sign, but regrettably, it does not make for happiness.

People who possess long **Mercury** fingers are, in the most modest circumstances, chatterboxes; and the most lofty, the world's great orators. In any event, they possess the gift of the gab and like to hold the floor (and usually do!). Not surprisingly, this characteristic is frequently found in the hands of politicians. If the finger leans forwards slightly, it shows an ability to overcome obstacles, but in general, the straighter the finger the better.

If the Mercury finger is unduly short, especially if it begins quite low down the palm, it points to an uphill struggle and a hard life. The holder of this sign is certainly able to make headway in life, but if seen in the left hand has had, or the right, can expect, little help from the outside.

A crooked Mercury finger is no more lovable a sign than any other finger that is naturally bent. Frequently you will find this idiosyncrasy showing up in both hands, and the meaning is a cold nature and a rather cunning disposition. If this sign shows up in one hand alone, (usually the left) it could mean that this person has been badly let down and finds it difficult to forgive and impossible to forget. Such an experience has left a permanent scar which manifests itself in a callous outlook on life.

The **thumb** is a peculiarly human feature, so it is hardly surprising that its form should reflect so much about us. Indeed, palmists in some parts of the world concentrate exclusively on the thumb for their readings, finding out all they need to know through this single digit. Seen as part of the whole picture made up by the entire hand, the thumb throws considerable light on the will, energy and intellect.

The most telling features of the thumb are its shape and proportions, its flexibility, its precise position in the hand and its length. The strength and relative size of the top two phalanges or sections indicate the balance between impulse and reason, the flexibility points to adaptability, while the position and length relate to intellect.

The top section of the thumb, the nail phalange, symbolizes strength of will, while the second section, between the first and second joints, shows powers of reason and logic. (The fleshy part of the thumb, called the Mount of Venus, concentrates on love and affection, and is discussed in a separate chapter on the Affection lines.) Dealing with will and reason first, we will compare two very different types of thumbs.

First there is the powerful sort of thumb, dominated by a very strong phalange of Will, with a comparatively weak, possibly waisted, phalange of Reason or Logic. This thumb denotes great resources of energy and vigour and, needless to say, considerable willpower. When the phalange of Reason is particularly weak, the implication is that the will takes over, and the subject acts on impulse, ignoring reason and restraint. A very strong phalange of Will is found in the hands of those people who always act at double speed, never hesitating before turning an idea into a reality.

People with more highly developed, thicker set phalanges of Reason, and comparatively weak phalanges of Will, are the great philosophers. Always giving very careful consideration to any project before putting a plan into action, these types never act hastily. They will weigh all the pros and cons in the balance, look at all aspects, listen to any amount of advice, before making a decision.

If the section of the thumb relating to Reason dominates the Will phalange, the powers of logic will be too highly developed and the subject will find it difficult to put plans into action at all. In this instance, the Will phalange will be seen to be rather weak. This is not a very good sign, showing someone who finds it difficult to stand on his or her own feet; possibly over-protected as a child, such a character is unlikely to make a forceful impression on the world.

A perfectly balanced thumb, with equal emphasis on each of these important sections (which, incidentally, is not so common as it sounds) indicates someone who has the ability to reason things out and is accustomed to pausing and thinking before acting.

Occasionally, you will see a very ugly looking – almost deformed – phalange of Will with a very bulbous finger print cushion and a rather wide, invariably short, deep set nail. This has been nicknamed the 'murderer's thumb', and does, indeed, have violent implications. Almost like a dominant phalange of Will gone wrong, it implies great resources of energy which find no natural channel.

Holders of such thumbs tend to vacillate between unnatural restraint and outbursts of temper (which are usually violent). If such a thumb is stiff, the outbursts will be extreme, and certainly murder could not be ruled out as one possible outcome of such rage. If a clubbed thumb is flexible, other channels will exist for the release of so much pent-up energy, and the consequences will not be nearly so violent or dramatic.

In general terms, the flexibility of the thumb is an important feature. Pliable thumbs, which naturally bend back a little of their own accord, and can easily be bent back further under very little pressure, show a broadness of mind and an easy-going nature. These are not quarrelsome types, they hate arguments, and would rather fall in with the consensus of opinion than make a stand on their own. A pliable thumb also means generosity; if it is too pliable, however, its owner is likely to be too pliable as well, easily led, profligately generous and tending to be decadently undisciplined as well.

Stiff thumbs, on the other hand, show those who are very set in their ways. These people tend to close their minds to anything new and obstinately continue on a predestined course. Because of their inflexibility, they can quite easily be roused and become argumentative if they do not get their own way. They not only set a hard régime for themselves, but also expect the same in others. Carefulness with money is just one obvious sign of their over-cautious streak.

On the subject of position and length, the ideal thumb is long, but not heavy, begins roughly halfway up the palm, and when the hand is closed, reaches almost up to the first joint of the Jupiter finger. This, the 'average' thumb, shows that the subject has a good brain and understands moderation.

An excessively long thumb does, in fact, imply excess. Certainly this subject will be intelligent, but also a little over experimental.

A shortish thumb, reaching to the middle of the first phalange of the Jupiter, or below, denotes indecision, an occasionally chronic inability (especially when coupled with a well-formed phalange of Logic) to make up one's mind.

The closest creatures to us in the animal world are the apes and the nearest they get to a human thumb is a small, weak, poorly formed digit set very low in the hand. A small, low set thumb, therefore, is seen as a mark of regression, and is a sign of poor intellect.

The mounts on the palm (the fleshy areas underneath the fingers, at the base of the thumb and on the outside of the hand) indicate certain character traits if they are raised, and others if they are virtually flat.

The **mount of Venus,** as the name would imply, is concerned with love, and criss-crossed with the Affection lines. If this mount is raised, and stands out prominently from the hand, it denotes a very warm, physical nature and points to a well developed capacity for love and lust. A low, insignificant mount of Venus, by contrast, indicates a rather chilly personality who does not depend too much on either mental or physical relationships with fellow human beings.

When the **mount of Jupiter** is well developed, you can assume that the owner of this feature has a pretty high regard for self, and an ambitious, often domineering, personality. If this mount seems to protrude above the others, arrogance and selfishness are implied. If, alternatively, the mount seems almost flat, the indication is that this person is rather diffident, not very positive and rather careless as a result.

If the **mount of Saturn** is more prominent than its peers, destiny will play a very important part in this person's life. Combined with a good brain and good vision, this can be a powerful sign.

A raised **mount of the Sun** is a very successful sign. It shows that abilities, in whichever field they may exist, will be put to good use, often bringing material gain.

The **mount of Mercury** is concerned with the business side of things, and when prominent it highlights aptitudes in this sphere. If it appears to be rather low, laziness and lack of ambition are implied.

The **mount of the Moon**, the ridge running down the outside of the palm, is associated with imagination and intuition. If it is well developed, standing proud of the palm, you can assume the subject has unusual flair for one of the arts (and, incidentally, probably a well-tuned sixth sense as well). A low mount of the Moon shows a pragmatic nature denoting lack of vision and a rather unsympathetic streak.

While we are on the subject of the mounts, just a word about the centre of the palm as well: although high mounts are generally desirable features to have, this should not be at the expense of the middle of the hand. A sunken palm (the area between the Life and Head lines sinking in like a valley) is a very unfortunate sign, showing that the subject has had, and always will have, to struggle through life. Ideally, although the mounts should be raised they should not overshadow the central plane of the hand.

5

THE PRINCIPAL LINES

THE LIFE LINE

People who have reservations about having their hands read are usually, no matter what their excuses may be, afraid of 'being told the worst'. They imagine that one glance at their Life line will reveal, with no shadow of doubt, the exact moment of their death. Of course this is not so! If it were, life assurance companies would not bother to ask for a medical report, but simply request hand prints instead.

Occasionally, it must be said, a very experienced palmist will, after considering *all* the lines in the palm, come to the conclusion that someone will not make old bones. But experience will also tell the palmist to keep such thoughts to him (or her) self. Only amateurs and charlatans blunder into predictions about death – and usually these cannot be trusted anyway. So before setting out to read anyone's palm, reassure them first that you will certainly not foretell any disasters.

Far from being a coup to act like a medieval witch and foretell nothing but gloom and doom, it is, incidentally, illegal in many countries to predict death, so even if you yourself have a morbid disposition, it is best not to acquire the habit. Foretelling the future is, after all, a positive rather than a negative pastime, and the Life line, as its name suggests, is a positive line.

It is, of course, concerned with life, with contentment and vitality, ambition and travel. And since it sweeps around the mount of Venus at the base of the thumb, it has something to do with love and affection as well. The starting point for the Life line is on the inside edge of the palm between the thumb and the base of the finger of Jupiter. The termination point of a long and complete Life line is at the first bracelet where the palm joins the wrist, anywhere under the fleshy mount of Venus.

The quality of the line, whether it is firm, clear and direct, or wiggly and wishy-washy says a lot about a person's constitution. The simpler, clearer and longer, the better; a short, faint or chained lined is a sign of delicacy and potential ill health. Ideally, the line should proceed unhindered by other lines or marks, and such a smooth, well-traced line shows strength, contentment, good health and good nature.

More often, of course, lines have their own idiosyncrasies: off-shoots, breaks and marks, and each of these has a story to tell, but only a complete story if you consider the similarities and differences between both hands.

If the Life line shows up to be weaker or shorter in the left hand than in the right, for instance, it could point to a childhood illness. In extreme cases, this illness could be serious, but evidence of greater strength and length of Life line in the right palm reveals that recovery was – or will be – complete. A break in the Life line in the right hand could, in the same way, point to an accident in later life. However, a strong and resolute Life line in the left hand shows that the subject is destined to live a long life, and live a long life he or she almost certainly will, either by conquering the effects of any accident – or by avoiding such an accident altogether.

So it can be seen that snap decisions can never be made about the Life line, since this important key to the hand is not nearly so straightforward as newcomers to the art of palmistry may think.

One positive feature worth looking out for is branches leaving the Life line, and the direction that they take. Any branches pointing upwards towards the fingers are a good sign to have. They denote endeavour and achievement, rewards and specific events. A line, for instance taking a firm path towards the finger of Jupiter is a sure sign of healthy ambition rewarded with personal success. Anyone holding this sign in his hand – or, better still, hands – is certain to improve his position in life.

A branch heading for the finger of Saturn reveals a more ruthless character; someone who will be a success, certainly (especially where material gains are concerned), but possibly by climbing over a few people on the way up. If the mount of Saturn is slightly raised, the chances are that this person will allow nothing to stand in the way of success, neither love, nor family, nor friends.

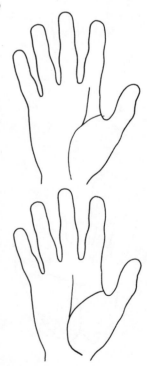

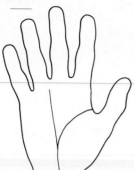

The finger and mount of the Sun are almost always associated with good fortune, and if a branch from the Life line points resolutely in this direction, its owner is destined for fame and acclaim.

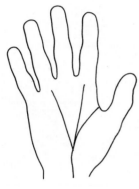

Two branches springing from the same place, one heading for the mount of Jupiter the other for the mount of the Sun, reveals the person who was born with everything one could want. Never having to strive for anything, the only thing lacking may be a sense of value and achievement.

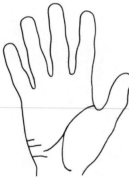

Lines branching downwards, away from the Life line and pointing towards the outside of the palm and the mount of the Moon, are associated with travel. These are usually found in hands already marked clearly with Travel lines, which have stories to tell in their own right (see page 63). The branches leaving the Life line endorse the urge to travel, and can point to a rather restless personality, always wanting to be on the move.

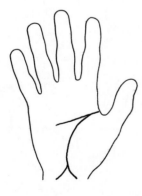

If the Life line itself terminates in a fork, with one branch curling round under the thumb, and the other pointing towards the base of the mount of the Moon, there is a strong possibility that the owner of this mark will end up actually living abroad. If the 'travel' branch leading towards the outside of the palm is the more clearly etched of the two lines, then emigration is almost a certainty. Sometimes (as illustrated) this sign will be seen in conjunction with the classic sign of dependence on family – the Life line and Head line running together for the first short stretch of life (see page 33); in this case, the subject could well be torn, straining to go away, while at the same time being held back by the family.

Breaks in this important line are dreaded by people who know little about palmistry. They seem to spell out clearly the interruption of the flow of life, but quite often they do not mean this at all. For instance, a break can have a repair line behind it, just a short way in towards the thumb. In this instance, the break itself could signify an illness, or possibly an accident, but the repair line considerably reduces its effect. In fact the event could be so minor that it could even pass without notice – particularly if the Life line in the other hand is long and strong.

Another guarantee of health is the square. If an apparent break is in fact boxed in by four other fine lines, these shield the subject at the time of the threat, and so minimize its effect.

If a break backed up with a repair line is bisected by a short, strong line heading out towards the centre of the palm, the meaning of the break can be quite different altogether. Certainly it will mean the cessation of life as you knew it before, but only because a whole new life is about to start. The holder of this mark could, for instance, be destined to uproot everything and move to somewhere entirely different, possibly overseas.

It could mean marriage; a marriage which would completely change his (or her) way of life. Or it could just mean that the subject will form a new association with someone who is very powerful, and has the will and the strength to alter the direction of his life.

To be sure of the meaning of this somewhat complex sign, it is necessary to look for other signals in the hand to support whatever conclusion you come to. If, for instance, a move overseas is implied, the Life line itself is likely to fork as it makes its way down the hand, one branch heading for the base of the mount of the Moon, and the other curling naturally round under the mount of Venus.

If you think marriage causes the change, look for corroboration in the Affection lines, and see if one particularly prominent line crosses the Life line and makes tracks up to the mount of Mercury. A strong association would show itself on the mount of Venus as well, probably crossing the Life line heading up towards the fingers, but stopping abruptly, either on reaching the Head or the Heart line.

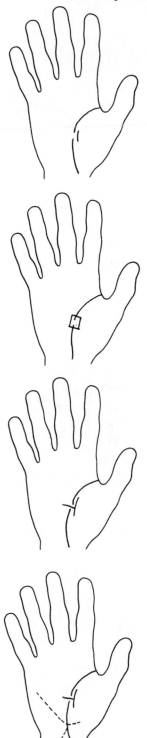

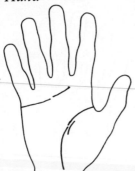

If you see a break in both Life lines at the same point, it is more than likely that there will be some sort of a physical setback at that time. If, however, the Head and Heart lines can be seen to proceed quite normally and not stop short, the effects of the misfortune will be overcome, and the subject will almost certainly make a complete recovery.

If the Heart line has a break in it at roughly the same point as the break in the Life line (backed up by the comforting little line of repair, that is), the meaning is a broken heart. But the owner should take comfort from the fact that both lines continue strongly beyond this miserable point, and a new start with somebody else can be foreseen.

Most of us have enough resilience to get over even major setbacks in life – although at the time this may seem quite impossible. If these two breaks are seen in a hand together with a Head line which slopes deeply down towards the wrist, however, the chances are that this person will feel the blow more painfully and lastingly than the majority, and will need – and should have – plenty of support during the difficult times.

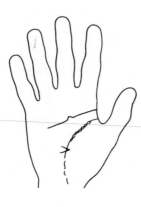

From the colour and clarity of the Life line, it is possible to deduce a little about the affections of the person whose hands are being read. In general, deeply etched lines, darker in colour than the palm itself, point to warm, outgoing characters who have an affectionate nature. Pale, shallow lines, on the other hand, infer distance, and are generally found in the hands of people who tend to keep even their close friends at arm's length.

Physical condition can show itself up quite clearly on the Life line, as indicated at the beginning of the chapter. Either continuous or patchy chaining on the line shows that someone is not all that robust. A line which begins clearly etched and becomes increasingly fragmented as it makes its way towards the wrist, shows that a person's health will deteriorate as he or she grows old. And a final clue to health is if the Life line is crossed by a V on its side. This is almost always a sign of poor eyesight, and in acute cases, the Head line will probably be humped as well.

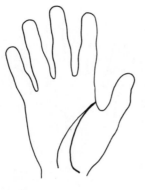

Finally, as rare as truly 'unhealthy' Life lines, are those which are a guarantee of good health and vitality. Holders of a double Life line live a charmed life. Although they may be threatened by illness and misfortunes like the rest of us, these will never really take their toll, because even if the principal Life line is threatened, the sister line is always waiting just behind to take the strain.

The primary motive force directing the course of a person's life is in his head, which is as good an explanation as any as to why the Head line is so illuminating when it comes to judging just what makes a person tick. Even if someone has numerous gifts, for instance, they are next to worthless if they do not also have either the drive or the ability to put them to good use.

The Head line, therefore, highlights not only the talents – even hidden talents – a person may have, but also their aptitude and ability. The more pairs of hands you look at, the more often you will find totally contrasting Head lines in both the left and the right hands. The combination of the two can be powerful, or you may see that the promise shown in one hand is not fulfilled in the other . . . The Head line indicates intelligence as well and, all too easily, mental instability. From it you can spot the dreamer, the introvert, the quick tempered, and even a subject likely to have criminal tendencies. Like the other important lines in the hand, however, the Head line should not be read in isolation.

The information it gives is only part of the complete picture. There will be many times when you are reading hands when you will find yourself having to refer back to the Head line from the other lines, because the Head line is the crucial link. No matter what you see in either the past or the future of the person whose hands are being read, this evidence must only be considered in the light of what the Head line has to say as well. If, for example, the Head line dips down towards the base of the hand, the subject will be a bit of a dreamer, incapable of concentrating on any one thing for long. Understandably, this will negate any signs of ambition and success found elsewhere in the hand.

The Head line, then, starts somewhere between the beginning of the Life line and the base of the finger of Jupiter, right from the inner edge of the palm, and traces its course towards the other side. There are two usual angles for the line, sloping slightly downwards or travelling more or less straight across.

The first consideration when reading the Head line, however, is where exactly the line begins. It may start, for instance, in conjunction with the Life line, the two setting off together for the first half-centimetre or so, before branching out to take separate courses of their own. This junction point signifies the family, and anyone showing this trait in their hands is likely to have led a sheltered childhood. When the lines run together very determinedly, you can bet that the person whose hands are being read is rather shy and reserved, someone to whom independence has come late.

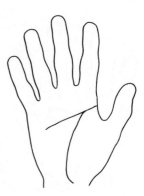

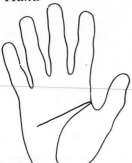

The person to whom independence comes – and has probably always come – easily shows a small gap between the commencement of the Life and the Head lines. This person is not afraid to stand alone. You will find that he or she is self-contained and a self-starter, and any burning ambitions are likely to be achieved without outside help.

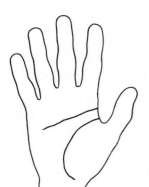

When the Head line starts much higher up, half way or more to the base of the finger of Jupiter, independence is carried to an antisocial extent. Instead of being healthily independent, this person is cold, selfish and potentially deceitful. Preferring their own company to that of others, people with this sign in their hands disdain not only other people, but animals as well. They have little sensitivity for the delicate pleasures of life; you would not, for instance, find this mark in the hand of any green-fingered gardeners.

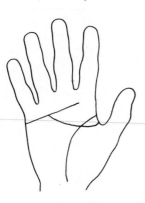

Occasionally, the Head line starts from inside the Life line itself, rising near the top of the mount of Venus. This is the sign of a rather grating character, quick to pick quarrels, slow to make friends. If the line continues to climb on an upward course, either running into, or cutting through the Heart line, the poor omens are compounded, and unless controlled, the quarrelsome nature can become either violent or potentially criminal.

The length of the Head line gives a good indication of a person's intelligence. The general rule is the longer the better, provided the line does not veer off on an undesirable course (i.e. swooping either down too low, or up too high). A good, straight line which traces its path across the hand, reaching over almost to the other side, is a mark of a great brain. This person has excellent powers of concentration and an unusual memory for details, even a photographic memory. Imagination may not be a strong point (unless this is revealed in the other hand), although logic is, making the subject an ideal candidate for any career concerning, for example, the law or a branch of science.

A shortish Head line, ending under the middle of the finger of the Sun, perhaps, indicates that the subject has a useful brain motivated by good common sense. This person is unlikely to be academically brilliant, however, and tending to lack initiative, would be better suited to being an employee than self employed.

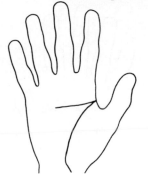

A very short Head line, ending under the finger of Saturn, is found in the hands of people of below average intelligence. In clear cut cases, the thumb, too, will be short, hardly reaching up to the base of the finger of Jupiter.

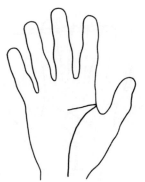

The course taken by the Head line as it makes its way across the hand inevitably has a number of things to add about the essential character of the person whose hands are being read. A straight Head line, which, without wavering, inclines very slightly down towards the wrist is held in the hand of an astute business person, with a keen brain for commerce. If the Heart line mirrors this shape, you can be sure that this subject is very capable and makes the most of his numerate abilities.

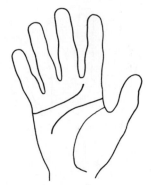

Sometimes a straight, strong Head line will deviate from its course in the centre of the hand, and tilt down towards the wrist. The deviation from course indicates an active imagination and certain artistic ability. Such a person could well work successfully in business during the day, but nevertheless look forward to returning home in the evenings to pursue a totally unrelated hobby such as painting, perhaps, or writing poetry. If this feature is found in the left hand alone, the artistic leanings, though latent, could well remain undiscovered; found only in the right, they could be chanced upon in later life.

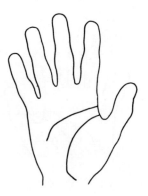

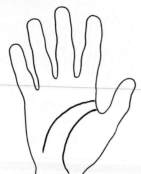

There is nothing wrong with a Head line that bends gently down towards the wrist. It simply shows that someone is very sensitive, a dreamer, probably someone who in the Sixties would have been a bit of a hippy. A long Head line sloping down to touch the mount of the Moon, low on the outside of the hand, denotes the true idealist. Artists in all fields tend to be more sensitive than most of mankind, and their artistic ability as well as their sensitivity will show up to a greater or lesser extent in accordance with the length and the slope of the line.

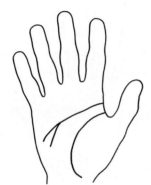

If a sloping Head line terminates in a fork, it suggests that the subject is prone to exaggerate. Coupled with a very long finger of Mercury, stretching up to the top phalange of the Sun finger, exaggerations can be taken to extremes, and turn into deliberate lies.

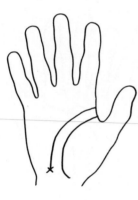

A line with an exaggerated slope towards the wrist is not a good sign. Altogether too sensitive, and too imaginative, for their own good, possessors of this sign at best tend to be the born worriers of the world, at worst mentally depressive, with possible suicidal tendencies. If such a Head line terminates in a cross, any suicidal feelings or threats should be taken very seriously.

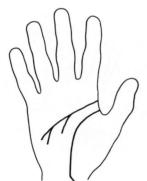

Any positive branches pointing deeply down towards the wrist from the Head line indicate worry and mental strain. A prominent, low plunging branch will be found in the hands of anyone who is either obsessed by his own worries, or preoccupied by the troubles of the world. This is quite logical when you consider that a mild downward dip denotes a strong imagination. If the imagination (and the dip) become too strong, a sensitive being finds it increasingly difficult to cope. Such a person could well become a recluse, unwilling to face the rigours of the outside world.

Hair lines sloping downwards from the Head line also show morbid tendencies, while we are on the subject, and indicate likely bouts of depression.

A downward sloping branch leaving the Head line and tracing its way back across the Life line on to the mount of Venus is rarely seen, and just as well, since it points to a difficult character, rather irritable by nature. Almost impossible to please, this type of person seems to revel in unhappiness and make a meal out of misery.

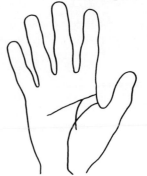

A regular fork at the end of a normal Head line, on the other hand, is an indication of a much more acceptable character trait, pointing towards artistic appreciation and literary ability. If the fork has three distinct prongs instead of two, it would appear that success is in store, and even within the person's life time, recognition and, possibly, honour.

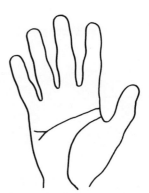

Lines branching upwards from the Head line, pointing definitely towards one finger or another, add more features to the picture of the subject whose character is being assessed. A line shooting off up towards the Jupiter finger points out the extrovert who has a taste for drama. Well suited to the stage, this person has a gift for acting and mimicry.

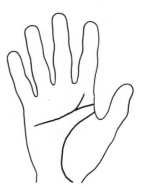

A shoot heading for the Saturn finger, however, has a very different meaning altogether. Someone carrying this mark will be found to have strong religious convictions and a leaning towards the church. Scientists, too, often display this sign, which signifies vocation, a real belief in the worth of the job in hand.

The Sun finger, is linked with good luck and prosperity. If a branch leaves the Head line and traverses this mount, it is indeed a fortunate sign, indicating success in whatever practical thing a person chooses to turn to. This branch is also a sign of originality, and aptly, is frequently found in the hands of those who take up any form of designing as a career.

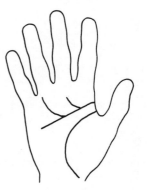

THE HEART LINE

Even at a first meeting you can judge how likeable a person is; whether he or she is humorous, shy, intelligent or attractive. But no one has the ability to see into another person's heart. No one can simply guess the answer to the ever-changing riddle of the unseen, perhaps unknown, emotions of a stranger, friend, lover, or even themselves.

The emotions are a powerful, uncontrollable force. Their strength, direction and motivation are a mystery to us all. To understand exactly what fires someone's heart, what makes them fall in love with a particular person at a particular time; or what makes them change course suddenly and drastically mid-affair would, let's face it, take a lot of the excitement and romance out of love.

But even the most sentimental of us must admit that to have just a clue as to what makes us all tick could save much agonizing and heartache and a lot of hit and miss affairs. Love is a rule unto itself and no amount of learning, no strength of will can force innermost feelings to be obedient and rational. Feelings make up their own rules as they go along, sometimes following a pattern, occasionally quite unpredictable. The only outward clue to how the hectic pendulum of the heart is likely to swing is the Heart line itself, and from this you can learn all sorts of secrets about a person's hidden nature.

You can tell, for instance, if someone is a 'good bet' in affairs of the heart; if their love and attentions are genuine, or merely a means to an end. You can spot the obvious flirt, the two-timer, the person who is obsessively jealous. Reading the Heart line in conjunction with the other relevant lines, you can tell if a relationship is destined to finish, and who is likely to initiate the split.

The Heart line can contain pointers towards health as well. That the emotions should – metaphorically at least – be assumed to stem from the organ whose job is to pump blood round the body may, when you think of it, seem a little unlikely. But the link is far more realistic than you might imagine. Intense emotional feelings do in fact exert a certain amount of pressure on the heart. Indeed to 'die of a broken heart' is a medical fact of life as much as it is a figurative one.

The Heart line in the hand, therefore, tells you not just about feelings of the heart meaning the emotions but about the working of the actual organ. Although a break in the line may indicate an irrevocable split in an important relationship (if other lines in the hand tell the same story, that is) it should not immediately be assumed that it means a heart attack as well. It does not, of course.

But experienced palmists can tell when the heart is under strain, for instance, and when it is a good idea to live life at a slightly more relaxed pace.

This Heart line, then, which reflects such important things about your life, runs from the outside of the palm, about an inch below the Mercury finger, making its way across towards the other side. It may either slope gently up towards the base of one of the other fingers, run straight across more or less parallel to the wrist, or incline down towards the thumb. The nature of the line itself, its direction and its character may throw light not only on mental attitude towards love but on physical proclivities as well.

First plotting its course across the hand, we will look at the meaning of its various termination points. In general, upward drift towards the fingers is the most desirable sign, and not only the main line itself, but its branches taking this course can give very favourable indications.

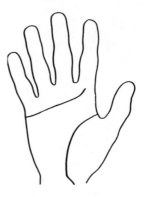

Take the line that plots its path across the hand to end in the middle of the mount of Jupiter under the index finger, for example. This is a very happy sign where partnerships are concerned, showing a kind-hearted, loving individual. Tolerant, sympathetic and loyal, sexually well-adjusted, the bearer of this line could even be too good to be true, sacrificing too much for love. Seen in the hand of a potential lover, beware until time has proved that the relationship is based on more than just romance and passion. People who hold this line in their hands may just fall in love too easily and too often for their own good. Combined with a few hair lines leaving the main line and branching up towards the fingertips, however, in general this sign indicates the best partner in marriage there is.

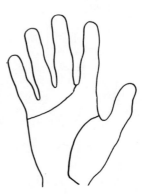

A line terminating between the fingers of Jupiter and Saturn, going right up to the top of the palm, is a sign of obsessive love and jealousy. Certainly having very strong feelings where love is concerned is only natural, and to an extent desirable. But if this love is too possessive, it can stifle not only relationships, but also ruin the private future of those concerned as well. However, this jealous streak can be controlled. This line is an indication of a trait which *could* exist in a person's nature; if they are aware of its existence they can start to try to temper their potentially possessive vein.

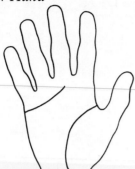

A Heart line which ends up on the mount of Saturn indicates a personality tending to be a bit over-cautious in romance. Found usually in the hand of a very orderly, regular type of person, who accepts routine willingly and has no quarrels at all with the nine-to-five predictability of his (or her) job, you have no romantic here! You can forget sentimentality, love letters, roses . . . but these aren't everything. Find someone with this sign in his or her hand, and you have found someone you can trust.

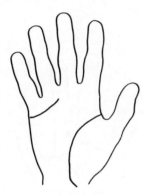

A very short Heart line terminating around the mount of the Sun is not common at all. Its bearer may well be very kind and well meaning but, as the brevity of the line would suggest, has a rather faint heart both physically and emotionally.

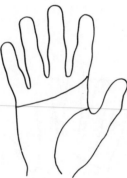

Occasionally, the Heart line makes its way right across the hand, from one side to the other, even curving round beyond the mount of Jupiter to the very edge of the palm itself. Seen together with a normal Head line this signals the egocentric; the person who is always out for him or herself. A good sign for business, perhaps, but a far less welcome sign in affairs of the heart.

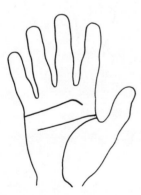

A Heart line reaching across the hand to beneath the mount of Saturn or Jupiter and then positively inclining down towards the Head line – though not touching it – is not a very lovable sign. It suggests that its owner is rather cold-natured, moody and difficult to get close to. This person is very hard to please; and wears a suit of armour in which you will find few chinks. Out for number one, particularly sexually, he or she expects no favours, and gives none. (This line, incidentally, is often found in the hands of bisexuals.)

When the Heart line extends down even further, and actually joins up with the Head line, it suggests a tendency to be violent, and if this downward sweep is reflected in the Head line itself as well, this tendency becomes acute. The point where the Life line and the Head line begin, between the thumb and the finger of Jupiter, symbolizes early childhood and the family. When the Heart line descends to strike this point, the violent streak could be directed either inwardly towards the self, or towards the immediate family.

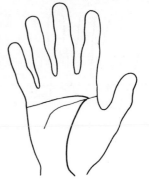

Before we move on to the meaning of the branches and fine auxiliary lines, let us look at the double Heart line, where there are two main parallel lines, both equally clear and well-etched, tracing their course side by side. This is the sign of great physical strength and of a great provider and spouse. Very devoted, home loving, and domesticated, here you have another sign of the ideal partner.

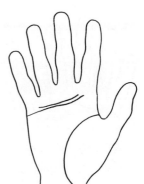

The rule concerning fine lines and branches attached to the Heart line is that those pointing upwards towards the fingers generally bring good news and those inclining down towards the wrist, bad. When the Heart line proceeding towards its termination point bursts into three branches shooting up towards the fingers, it indicates a very artistic nature. This sign is frequently found in the hands of writers, poets, playwrights and artists, and also, though less obviously, doctors. Sexually and emotionally, holders of this sign tend to be loyal, despite constant attentions from the opposite sex, and repeated temptations to stray.

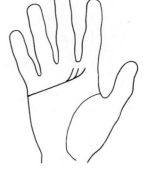

Three branches looking like a fan or tassle, bursting in all directions out of the end of the line, denote ambition and success. Down to earth types, the bearers of this sign are reliable, good listeners and have a lot of friends. They are warm and apparently unassuming, but behind this affable, lovable exterior, there is hidden drive and persistence, which will undoubtedly bring success in the end. Where love is concerned, usually this sign is associated with an unhappy experience – perhaps the subject has been, or is afraid of being, let down – and is therefore rather diffident. He or she tends to crave love but mistrust it when it comes.

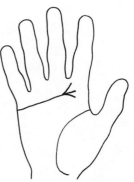

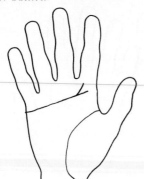

A Heart line which ends in a tassle or fan and also bears a branch going straight up over the mount of the Sun, indicates an excellent partnership and a true marriage of minds.

The simple forking of a Heart line into two distinct branches at the end can reveal that you have – or will have, if the sign exists in the right hand alone – two people in your life. Usually this sign is associated with weighty decisions and a very difficult choice.

Branches and hair lines often mean new or different affairs. If a Heart line resembles a feather, with many hair lines bristling out on both sides, you have in front of you the hand of a flirt. This person is literally on the look out – and being looked out for – all the time. Wooing has become a full-time job, and it must be said that the tactics which have been developed to make multiple conquests possible may sometimes be cruel. The feather effect, however, may be concentrated in the early part of the Heart line and after a point the line may proceed without hair lines and branches. This indicates that happiness with one partner is achieved after a spell of ruthlessly 'playing the field'.

Hair lines sloping downwards towards the Head line reveal disappointments in love; in the left hand disappointments in the past, in the right yet more in the future. People so apparently dogged by misfortune cannot simply blame bad luck. Like as not there is something in their nature which brings disappointments to others as well as to themselves. Perhaps they find it difficult to be sufficiently single-minded about one relationship to make it work. Jealousy could be the wrecker – indicated by the heart line tracing its way right up between the fingers of Jupiter and Saturn. Or selfishness, perhaps, which shows up either in a very hard, ungiving palm, or in a Heart line which dips slightly down towards the Head line under the finger of Jupiter.

A series of upward sweeping branches leaving the Heart line towards its termination point is a sign of good fortune. Found in the left hand they intimate that their owner has never wanted for anything. Through no effort of his own, this person has always been lucky enough to be given what he wants. Found in the right hand only, these branches signify events; their owner is bound to have an exciting life, but potentially a complicated one. This sign is usually found in soft hands with tapering fingers, and in classic cases, points to someone who, on the face of it, has everything. Below the surface, however, don't forget that feelings of inadequacy and self-doubt could lurk as well.

A Heart line with two single branches shooting up to the bases of the fingers of Jupiter and Saturn is a very lucky sign. It points to luck in love, a successful and fulfilling partnership and the achievement of most personal ambitions.

If fortunate, upward-growing branches are counterbalanced by a very definite fork which plunges down across the Head line to the Life line, all personal potential and achievement is stultified by the strong influence of either the family, a partner or, in rare instances, a powerful friend. Such a person in the life of the holder of this sign holds him back, and however strong his ambition, his will to succeed, even his good luck, its presence will act as a brake.

The gap between the Heart line and the Head line, whether it is wide (about a centimetre or more) or really quite narrow, has a thing or two to say as well, reflecting attributes such as humour, sociability and guile. It is important to take the gap into account when reading all the other implications of the lines, because it could well accentuate the meaning or detract from it. For further explanation of the meaning of this gap – called the Quadrangle – see Chapter 6.

Sometimes a line or lines may break off from the Heart line to join up with the Head line, and in extreme cases, the two lines blend into a single line traversing the whole width of the palm. This single line is known as the Simian line, because it is a characteristic of other primates, principally monkeys and gorillas.

Owners of this sign are usually attributed with a fairly fundamental outlook on life, abiding more by the laws of the jungle, than deferring to the niceties of civilized society. It is very rare for this sign to show up in both hands, but if it does, beware! It is believed to be an outward and visible sign of regression and degeneracy, and indicates the kind of unruliness and irresponsibility usually found only among those with criminal tendencies. Owners of Simian lines in both hands are not really suited to partnerships of the heart, since they find little comfort in the everyday pleasures enjoyed by the rest of us, making up their own rules as they go along . . . on their own. This sign is, however, very rare. Slightly more common is an incipient or fully-fledged Simian line showing up in one hand alone.

In the left hand, it shows someone who has led a very sheltered early life, never having to take responsibilities for himself. In adulthood, this person is likely to shun responsibility, choosing the easiest way out of most situations. The holder of this line is a person of a single great passion, which may be a hobby, a career, or a great love, and everything else in life will be sacrificed to this one ideal. If you are involved with the bearer of a Simian line and you are not this one ideal, forget it – you will always take second place.

Seen only in the right hand, the Simian line indicates that a man or woman grew into the single-minded being that they are. Often fired by unusual sexual drive, they tend to concentrate more on the physical than the emotional side of love.

The quality of the Heart line, whether it is strong and straight, a bit wiggly, chained or dotted, also has some information to add. The healthiest lines are straight and clear, reflecting not only the health of the heart, but the clarity of the emotions, and the stamina of the sex drive too. The wavy line shows up in the hand of the vacillator, who just does not know what he really wants. One minute he decides on one course of action, the next, another. Chaining, either in patches or continuously, shows when undue strain is being put on the heart. At an emotional level, it can be a sign that its owner is untrustworthy, too easy-going for his or her own good, and found in conjunction with a large gap between the Heart line and the Head line, points to someone who is potentially extremely lazy.

The deeper and more definite the Heart line, the stronger the heart, both physically and emotionally. This sign is usually held in the hands of strong, warm, lovable and loving individuals (who have the healthiest sex drive too, incidentally) and is the best sort of Heart line to have.

Paler, weaker lines point to a more delicate constitution and tend to show that the subject tires easily and should not undertake strenuous work as it could put a strain on a rather weak chest. In affairs, people with faint Heart lines are reliably monogamous and loyal. If a sister line (however faint) is seen running alongside a pale Heart line, the weakness of the principal Heart line is bolstered and the sister line acts as a kind of insurance policy, injecting additional strength (both physical and emotional) when required. Dots on the Heart line are never a good sign and can point to a period of ill health.

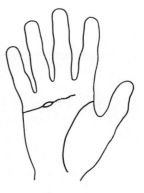

An island on the Heart line (see page 78) suggests a break in a partnership, the end of an affair or a radical change of heart where an important relationship is concerned. The Affection lines, discussed in the next chapter, should shed more light on the exact nature of the disturbance, and if a split is implied, will indicate who is the instigator.

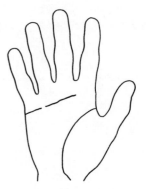

Breaks in the Heart line mean many different things: an emotional trauma, the end of an affair, a self-initiated change of events or even an illness. A great number of subjects who proffer their hands to be read do so because they are both fascinated to hear the good news . . . and have a morbid interest in hearing the worst. A break seems to the uninitiated to spell catastrophe, and it is very important that the reader first reassures the anxious holder of a broken Heart line that it need mean nothing serious at all before carefully examining not only both hands individually, but also looking for other signs in the hand which will throw more light on the meaning of the break.

6

THE MINOR LINES

THE LINE OF DESTINY

The line of Destiny is something of a vocational line; it can give a sense of purpose to many different areas of the subject's life. Acting like a kind of accelerator pedal, it underlines its owner's willpower, drive and initiative, and highlights an inner ability to channel both energies and talents appropriately.

Not every hand has a line of Destiny, however. Sometimes it is totally missing from both hands, which is not a sign that there is 'something lacking', only an indication that someone has to work harder to carve out a comfortable, purposeful niche in life. Those people without Destiny lines are not fired by the same single-mindedness of purpose as holders of this sign.

Those who have a line of Destiny in each hand, however, will very rarely have two identical lines, because something so difficult to define as inner resolution will seldom remain absolutely constant throughout life. Sometimes you will see a very strong line of Destiny in the left hand and virtually nothing in the right, showing that the inner drive exists latently, but has never really come into its own. (Reverse this rule, of course, for left handed people.) A well-etched line of Destiny in the right hand, which is not reflected in the left, is a much more positive and powerful sign, showing that this hidden motive force comes into its own in adulthood.

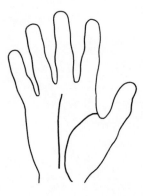

The 'prototype' line of Destiny, travelling straight up the centre of the palm from the wrist to the mount of Saturn, shows an unusual ability and will to succeed. This sign is held in the hands of someone who is destined to make a go of things; a person with unusual powers of concentration and determination, who becomes totally involved in anything and everything. A sense of vocation, often, is the motive force and fulfilment results from a sincere love of life, including work.

If the line is over-long, going right up to the base of the finger of Saturn, and even beyond, the precious gift of energy and willpower becomes almost too concentrated to be of value. Someone bearing this mark has so much drive that instead of enhancing such gifts and potential, he or she eventually mars them by going just too far. This mark is held in the hands of workaholics and those who allow their interests to become obsessions.

When the line of Destiny begins half way up the hand, the inference is that the subject took a long time to find his way. Perhaps he (or she) got off to several false starts, couldn't settle on a particular course, was a little behind with the process of self-knowledge. The point when the line starts to show marks the moment when everything begins to fall into place; a new awakening, and probably the start of a new career.

If the line of Destiny springs from the Head line, making its way firmly up the hand from there, this inner resourcefulness and energy is latent until later in life, when it is released only by using logic and intelligence. Holders of this mark are self starters, who need to have gathered a certain amount of confidence and experience before they dare to branch out on their own.

In rare cases, the line of Destiny remains dormant until the Heart line, right at the top of the hand, when it springs into life. In this instance, any form of career or life's work is of secondary importance until nudged into prominence by an affair of the heart, probably marriage. Many people need the support of a partner to forge ahead and follow their ideals. Certainly someone with such a modestly short line of Destiny as this will have had a job or career earlier in life – and a successful one, too, in all possibility – but the sudden appearance of the line of Destiny nudges this job, or an interest or hobby, on to a different plane.

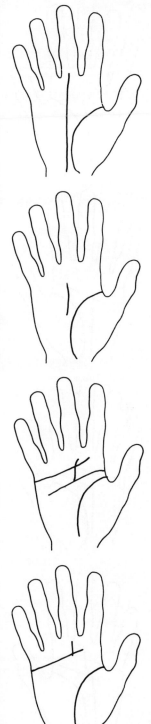

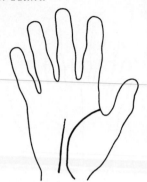

A line of Destiny springing from the base of the hand at the wrist and tailing off in the centre of the palm, implies that early drive and sense of direction are later shelved, for one reason or another. In female hands, the explanation is usually that career and time-consuming interests are dropped for a time, in favour of bringing up a family. In male hands, the cessation of the line of Destiny can point to a change of heart. A conscious decision to leave the rat race, perhaps, brought about either by a shift of ideals, or possibly by ill health.

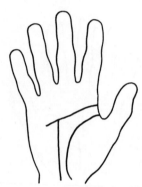

When the line comes to an abrupt halt when it reaches the Head line, it can mean that stubbornness of one sort or another prevents progress. Although the ingredients are all there, they are thwarted finally by a lack of vision and the reluctance to take risks.

The termination of the line of Destiny when it reaches the Heart line, shows that either a relationship or marriage stands in the way of the achievement of the current goal, whether it be the pursuit of an ideal, an interest or a career. This outside influence starts to control the subject's destiny, for better or for worse, altering the pattern of life.

Very often the line of Destiny is broken, meaning that the subject steps back to reassess his or her life at one time or another. If, after the break, the line continues on the same course, it means that after a breather, life resumes in the same vein; if however the line takes up its position somewhere else in the hand after the break, the meaning is a total change of direction.

If the line of Destiny ends in a fork or a fan at the top of the hand, the meaning again is a change in the course of life at one time or another. This change usually revolves around the career.

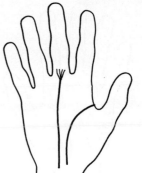

If the line of Destiny bears a branch heading towards the finger of Mercury, and this branch develops a fork at its termination point, a change in residence is implied.

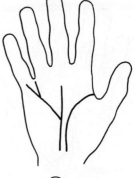

Instead of carving its way straight up the palm, the line of Destiny can spring from other parts of the hand; for instance it can come from inside the Life line, from the mount of Venus, finding its source among the Affection lines. This shows that a person's whole destiny is in the hands of the family, who will direct the course of his or her life and career.

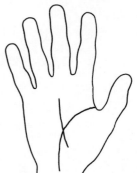

If the line of Destiny stems from the Life line itself, the meaning is quite different. This person makes his or her own way. Entirely self-motivated, he will forge ahead courageously, often against odds, following a vocational course. Usually the chosen career is less a job, more a way of life, and so dedication to it is only natural, and far from being a chore. This mark is often a sign that a person has the right temperament for being self-employed.

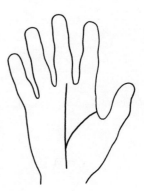

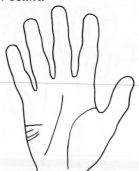

When this elusive line has its source on the outside of the palm, close to the Travel lines, travel is usually one of the greatest motivations in life. Either through work or pleasure, you can bet that someone carrying such a line gets around a lot and allows travel to shape the course of his life.

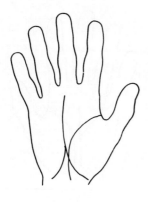

Occasionally, the line of Destiny has roots in both the mount of Venus and the mount of the Moon on the outside of the palm, forming a definite inverted V. This shows someone with great versatility, who not only has talents in different areas, but also the ability to put them to good use. An added meaning of this inverted V, if it forms a triangle with the first bracelet of the wrist, is the likelihood of inheritance.

THE SUN LINE

The Sun line has also been called the line of Apollo (because Apollo is another name for the Sun finger) and the line of Success, because it has to do with achievement, with fame, with material wealth and the fulfilment of wishes. By no means do all hands have Sun lines because, understandably, not everyone's life is geared towards achievement and success. And not all Sun lines are equally long and strong.

To judge the quality of the Sun line, it is necessary to compare its clarity with that of the other lines. A 'good' Sun line need only be good in comparative terms; i.e. if the major lines are all pretty weak, a faint Sun line can be considered to be quite strong.

The termination point of the Sun line is either on the mount of the Sun, or heading in this direction lower down in the hand. It may begin at the wrist, from the centre of the palm, from the Head line, from within the Quadrangle, from the Heart line, or even start and end on the mount of the Sun itself. The length has less significance (although it is relevant, of course) than the clarity of the line.

And the clarity and depth of the line bear a direct relationship to the potential success – material and personal – of the holder of the line. All over the hand there are possible signs of artistic talents, of drive and ambition and of business acumen. But it is to the Sun line that you look to find out if the promise is likely to be fulfilled.

This line, like so many of the minor lines in the hand, can change considerably in a comparatively short space of time. It can suddenly appear, various fragmented lines can, in time, blend together to form a single strong line, a break can first be patched up by the appearance of a sister line, before being mended altogther, and a strong line can, occasionally, almost fade out. So interestingly, the Sun line can be read topically, being pertinent on the day that it is studied. If it shows up clearly, as a straight, firm line, achievement of the goal in hand is assured.

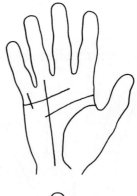

A long Sun line, stemming from as low down the hand as the bracelet dividing the palm from the wrist and making its way up to the mount of the Sun, shows a huge potential for success, public acknowledgement and fame. Elsewhere in the hand there will be pointers to the field in which the accolade is won: the arts, business, politics, the law. If the long, strong Sun line has a parallel line running up to the mount of Mercury, considerable financial rewards can be expected as well.

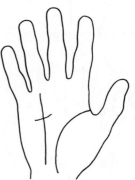

If a long Sun line, running up from the wrist, is crossed by a short, independent line, either when it reaches the centre of the palm or within the Quadrangle, the subject has either already received, or can expect, a financial windfall of some sort. Frequently this golden egg involves not just money, but property as well. If the Sun line continues firmly beyond this point, the implicit achievement is undoubtedly spurred along by the material boost.

A long Sun line running the length of the palm is seen less often than shorter versions which are normally found near the top of the hand.

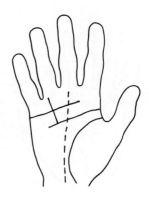

When the Sun line begins from the Head line, the indications are that the subject reaches his goal on his own merits. This line is frequently accompanied by a good line of Destiny in the hands of self-starters – the energetic, independent types who have the willpower to push ahead.

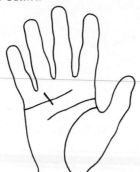

Short but clearly marked Sun lines starting either from within the Quadrangle or from the Heart line, do not mean that success will be diminished because of the brevity of the line. Often these short ines are the most topical, becoming very deep and clear when the impact of one sort or another is about to be – or has just been – felt.

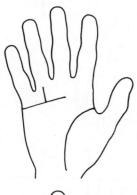

Heading up from the Heart line across the mount of the Sun towards the Sun finger in a purposeful way, the short Sun line shows that the subject is, or will shortly be, comfortably off for money. One irony here is that frequently people of subnormal intelligence, those whose brains are unable to progress beyond childhood, hold in their hands healthy Sun lines. The reason for this is that such people are invariably cared for by someone else, and are, in effect, often comfortably off.

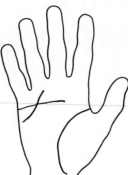

If the Sun line makes its way towards the Sun finger from beneath the mount of Mercury, success will be achieved through a partnership.

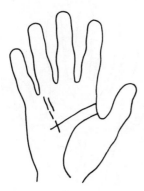

The clearly etched Sun line in almost any guise is associated with achievement and success. If it reveals a very obvious break, or even a series of breaks, the implication is that there will be a hindrance or several disappointments along the way. Where finances are concerned, this break implies the mismanagement of money and, if the break is very definite, even potential bankruptcy. But there could be a sister line running either parallel to the break, or parallel to the Sun line itself as it crosses the mount of the Sun, and this line will to a certain extent repair the damage. In money matters, the sister line indicates that losses will be replenished and total disaster averted.

The Sun line on its own is a sufficient sign of the granting of wishes – at least where material considerations are concerned. Unfortunately its significance only diminishes if there are several parallel lines heading up across the mount of the Sun towards the Sun finger. This sign points to the dilettante, who aspires towards many goals at once, and succeeds in reaching none.

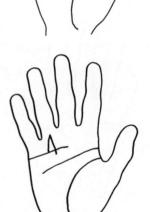

A Sun line which ends in a fork or a fan reveals that the potential for success exists, but is marred by a rather mercurial attitude. Through lack of concentration, the subject will be prone to shelving one job in favour of another – and ending up getting neither done. If a person holding this mark can be persuaded to adopt a more single-minded attitude, not only will much more be achieved, but also, the auxiliary lines will begin to fade.

If two lines on the mount of the Sun converge into one, to form a peak under the finger, happiness and the fulfilment of long-term wishes come to the subject late in life.

When the Sun line is chained, no matter how much effort is put into a project, little progress will result. This is rather an unfortunate and frustrating sign, but anyone who holds it should not be too discouraged, because the chaining can fade, and the line become clean and positive.

If the Sun line is hardly discernible, it certainly casts no shadow over the happiness of the person in question, but does indicate that progress on any practical level is likely to be slow at the current time. Faint lines can, if appropriate, firm up and will certainly do so if either luck, or circumstances, alter sufficiently.

MARRIAGE LINES

Only two things are certain in this life, so the saying goes – death and income tax. And palmistry, thank goodness, has little to do with either. Palmistry is not a science of the dead cert, but the subtle art of the possible. Your hands will show the ingredients, sometimes the quantities, and a little flavour of the taste. But they are certainly not going to be so blatant – and boring – as to show you the whole finished cake.

And so understanding the lines on your hands will not answer the question 'Will I marry Bill Bloggs next December?' Who you marry, and when (unlike death and income tax), is in your own control – in your own hands, if you like – and although the lines can tell the past and future of the main influences, partners and affairs, they will not predict what you will do with your own free will.

Marriage lines, therefore, serve only as pointers. When read together with other major lines – the Heart line, for instance – they offer quite a clear picture, but diminish none of the thrill of surprise.

Between the beginning of the Heart line and the base of the little finger, in that centimetre or so on the outside of your palm, there may be one, two or more short, but clear lines tracing their way towards the middle of your hand. These are known as the Marriage lines, although if several are present, not all, you will be relieved to hear, indicate different marriages. Strong family ties can also show up here, as well as important partnerships, which do not necessarily result in a piece of paper and a plain gold band. To distinguish between the different meanings of the lines, other patterns in the hand must be considered as well.

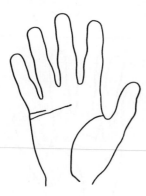

A dominant Marriage line, pointing straight across towards the opposite side of the palm means marriage, and if it appears in the same position on both hands, the timing of the marriage can roughly be judged. The nearer the Heart line the Marriage line appears, the younger the subject will be (or have been) when married. A third of the way up towards the finger of Mercury, the age will be about thirty or so, two thirds of the way up, sixty, etc. A straight, clearly defined line extending well into the mount of Mercury suggests a strong and lasting emotional link, and a stable partnership.

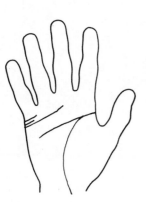

To see if a lesser Marriage line in fact points to a close family bond, look at the beginning of the Head line for additional proof. If the Head line and the Life line start together, it means that this person comes from a close family and is, if not ruled, at least strongly influenced by home, and could well make a late marriage.

If the weaker Marriage lines in fact mean powerful and lasting affairs, look for proof on the mount of Venus. The lines which fan out towards the Life line are Affection lines, the stronger ones of which indicate past and future emotional and sexual encounters. The lines which are deepest etched, are obviously the most important, and could well be echoed, as they should rightfully be, among the Marriage lines, especially if an Affection link makes its way tentatively across from the mount of Venus to the mount of Mercury (see Affection lines, pages 59–60).

Getting married is not, of course, an end in itself, but a beginning, and the palm naturally throws some light on the sort of marriage you are likely to make; whether it will be happy, if it will end abruptly, the aspects of your own character likely to put the relationship in jeopardy. . . Other lines in the hand of course throw light on the emotions and the nature of your intimate relationships, but there are patterns specifically concerned with marriage as well.

Held in the palm of the hand, there can be several different secret signs of a happy relationship, which should be pleasing and comforting to anyone who finds them there. For instance, if a strong Marriage line makes its way out into the hand towards the mount of the Sun, happiness and contentment are pretty well assured.

Another fortunate sign is if the principal Marriage line makes its way out across the mount of Mercury to meet up with the Sun line, forming an L. The Sun line, as its name would suggest, is a happy, sunny line to have, and if it links up with another line, it will shine benevolently on this aspect of a person's life as well.

A strong Marriage line held in the same hand as a cross on the mount of Jupiter, means that great happiness will be found in love and in a partnership which will be a success in every respect, emotional as well as social.

A star on the mount of Jupiter denotes consummate happiness and if other signs in the hand agree, a joyous marriage will be an important part of the Utopia.

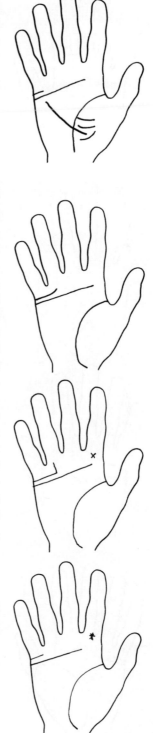

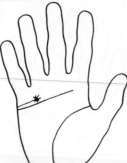

If the Marriage line itself ends in a star (a bit like a stylised drawing of a rocket) the subject's partner will have been born with exceptional abilities and will know how to make the most of these gifts, gaining recognition and acclaim for them both.

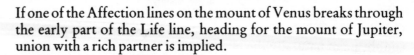

If one of the Affection lines on the mount of Venus breaks through the early part of the Life line, heading for the mount of Jupiter, union with a rich partner is implied.

A fact of life – and of palmistry – is that one is just as likely to find bad things around the corner as good. Although people may be able to keep the stormy side of their life hidden from relations and friends, they will not be able to keep the facts from showing up in their hands. Past, present and future upheavals show themselves in a number of different ways. You can foresee times of trouble and stress, separation, divorce, remarriage, and even widowhood. But do not be afraid to look either in your own hands, or be too wary of upsetting someone who proffers their hands to be read. It may well be necessary to overcome, or avoid, even the unlucky things you may spy before the subject can find the right road to happiness.

If the character of the principal Marriage line is in itself wavy, this is a fair indication of uncertainties. Coupled with a long Heart line stretching up to finish between the first and second fingers the weakness could well be caused by jealousy, which if not controlled, will put the whole future of that partnership in jeopardy.

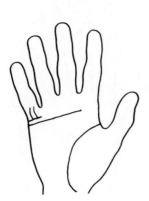

If the Marriage line joins up with the Child or Children lines (see page 63), it is a clear indication that the offspring are more important than the union itself, which is often not the healthiest sign.

A grille, as opposed to the quite distinct Children lines, crossing the Marriage lines signifies a rough ride at some stage – not disastrously rough, but just rather uncomfortable.

If the hand shows two parallel Marriage lines set quite close together, one more deeply etched than the other, but both bending inwards to join up in the shape of a pencil, the evidence is that there will be a break in the partnership, a temporary separation. This sign is often seen in the hands of servicemen or businessmen and women who have to go away for long spells because of work, for instance. The break can sometimes be voluntary, specially designed to give a rift in the partnership time to heal, but more often it is unavoidable, a fact of life, a duty to family or to work. The parallel Marriage line is a good sign, though, and means the relationship will resume later on, probably no worse, and if anything better off, for the break.

A Marriage line which begins strongly at the outside of the hand and gradually fades out is an indication that one or other of the partners will sooner or later (and this can roughly be judged by the length and strength of the line) leave home. There may well be no divorce, but to all intents and purposes, the marriage will cease to exist.

Divorce is indicated in quite a different way. A strong Marriage line which grows branches as it traces its way across the mount of Mercury is the sign of divorce. The branches represent another person – or other people – coming into the marriage, upsetting the status quo. If another strong Marriage line is in evidence above the version with branches, and if it is a 'clean' line, without forks, this second relationship stands a good chance of being entirely happy.

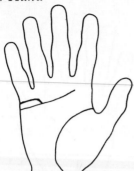

A Marriage line which dips down to join the Heart line reveals the fact that you will outlive your partner. This may well be in the fullness of time, and is nothing to become over-concerned about – in the same way as a straight line means that your partner will outlive you. One or other of these eventualities must happen, after all.

AFFECTION LINES

Usually the softest, most voluptuous part of the hand is the cushion-like mount at the base of the thumb, known as the mount of Venus. And quite suitably, this soft, comfortable quarter of the hand is associated with affection, love and physical passion. There are many pointers in the hand to relationships, to powers of affection and to appetite and energy for sex. And here all three are revealed.

First, before discussing the various lines and trends, however, the characteristics of the mount itself must be judged. A prominent mount, raised higher than any other part of the palm, implies a very sensuous nature, which needs and ceaselessly seeks out physical outlets for emotion. You will find few cold fish with well developed mounts of Venus; this feature being confined to the hands of warm, physically active types.

A shallow mount of Venus, on the other hand, is more likely to be found in the hand of idealists and philosophers, who are more likely to think, to ponder and to dream than to act.

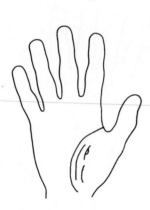

The lines on this almost hemispherical mount all relate in some way to relationships; relationships to family, to friends and to lovers. The lines following the curve around the thumb, running parallel to the Life line, all relate to ties with relatives. Some can be seen to be deeper and clearer than others, and you may notice islands, breaks, wiggles and other irregularities. These, however, are all part of perfectly normal family life.

The only judgement to be made is how clearly, in relation to other minor lines in the hand, these markings show up. If they are very well etched, and seem to stand out as one of the most important features of the hand, it can be assumed that the subject has kept close ties with the family. Rather weak lines reveal more independence and apathy to kith and kin, and could well be found in conjunction with a clear space between the beginning of the Head and Life lines.

People seeking to have their palms read are in general less interested in such facts as 'links with family', however, than they are in liaisons and affairs of the heart. So you are likely to find much more fascination in your interpretation of the other lines on the mount, those running from the thumb towards the Life line, since these have to do with links formed through love.

The Affection lines, as we call them, at their shallowest reflect close friendships, and at their deepest, important love affairs. A heavily marked network of these Affection lines points to someone who is not only attracted, but also attractive to the opposite sex. Sometimes you will sense that a person holding a great number of Affection lines has a highly developed appetite for physical and emotional conquests. Occasionally, however, clear Affection lines relate less to reality than to figments of the subject's imagination, the associations taking place only in the mind. But in most cases where plenty of Affection lines are apparent, you can assume that the subject either will, or already has, seen a thing or two of life. Looking in the right hand, you find the relationships of the present and of the future. An affair which is either already in progress, or just about to begin, will reveal itself as a very clearly marked line.

If the line remains within the area confined by the Life line, the affair, however important it may appear at the time, could well never go any further than that.

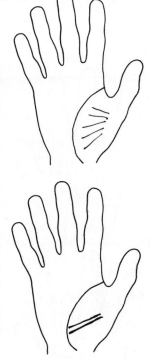

If two lines of apparently equal depth exist side by side, there could be a second person of importance in the subject's life, and running two affairs at once would naturally prevent either relationship from progressing too far. The second person might, however, only be a figment in the subject's mind: or someone already known, perhaps, but someone whose status is not yet that of a lover.

When an affair really blossoms, and starts to move forward on to a more concrete footing, the Affection line starts to extend in length, and moves out to cross the Life line.

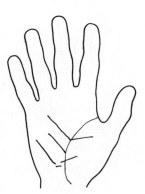

The lengthening of the Affection line is usually accompanied by the formation of an Affection *link*, which traces its way from the mount of Venus diagonally across the hand in the direction of the mount of Mercury (and, incidentally, the Marriage lines). The link may either be an extension of the Affection line itself, be joined to it by a bridge, or make its way independently across the palm.

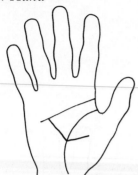

The Affection link reveals in its formation quite a bit about the nature of the relationship. If, for instance, it starts clearly, but stops abruptly on reaching the Head line, the implication is that obstacles crop up to mar the happy progress of the union. The obstacles could be the parents on either side, or someone else who interferes and claims to 'know best'. The cessation of the line shows that either the subject or the partner would rather wait than forge ahead and offend the third party. The situation is likely to be rather an uncomfortable one, and the subject is liable to feel torn.

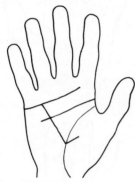

If the Affection link stops when it reaches the Heart line, it usually means that the other partner is already married, and therefore is unable to take the relationship to its natural conclusion.

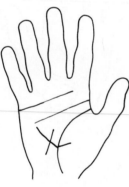

If an Affection link making its way diagonally across the palm up towards the mount of Mercury is crossed by a strong line heading from the mount of the Moon towards the mount of Jupiter, the subject decides to terminate the affair when ambition gets the better of affection.

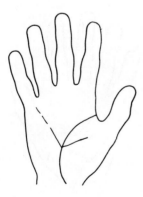

Breaks in the Affection link mean just that: breaks in the relationship. A stormy but intense courtship will show up in the hand as a fragmented Affection link. If the line none the less travels the full distance to the mount of Mercury, marriage could still be the outcome. A very powerful line which shows a single break and then resumes again, tells of a short, but important split; perhaps while one or other party goes off to decide about the best outcome for the relationship. From the strength of the line after the break, the likely outcome can be predicted.

If an Affection link heading for the mount of Mercury ends in a hook pointing down towards the mount of the Moon, the relationship will not end in marriage. Instead, it will terminate quite abruptly, and the subject will be responsible for – and happy with – the split.

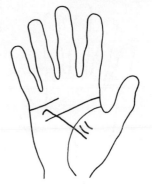

If an Affection link on its way to the mount of Mercury terminates in a cross, again the end of the current affair is implied. This time, the subject's partner is responsible for the rift, which could come as a bit of a shock. If, on the other hand, the Affection link runs its full course and reaches the mount of Mercury, marriage is definitely the outcome of this relationship.

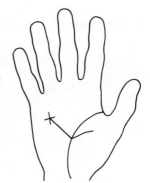

An Affection link leaving the mount of Venus, and crossing the Life and Head lines on its way to the mount of Jupiter points to an association with a rich and successful member of the opposite sex. The outcome of this liaison is likely to be a happy and fulfilling marriage.

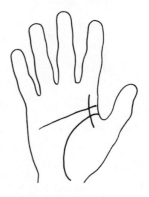

An Affection link travelling straight from the mount of Venus to the mount of the Moon, where you find the Travel lines, signifies a strong and lasting bond with someone who lives abroad, or with a foreigner. If this line is combined with a pronounced fork at the bottom of the Life line, all signs point to the union becoming permanent and being based abroad.

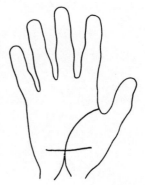

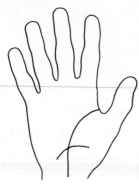

This particular sign should not be confused with a bowed line running from the mount of Venus, curving upwards towards the centre of the palm, and back down on to the mount of the Moon, since this arc has quite a different meaning altogether. This is called the Addiction line, since it is found in the hands of people who tend to rely too heavily on either drink or drugs. Found only in one hand, the condition may well not be acute. But seen in both hands, the implications are that the subject is some sort of addict.

An island on an Affection link denotes jealousy, probably on the part of the subject if the Heart line pushes its way up between the fingers of Jupiter and Saturn. If this auxiliary sign is not present in the subject's hand, then the jealousy is probably the fault of the partner instead.

CHILDREN LINES

From early childhood, girls are fascinated by the imponderable question of whether or not they will have children and, if so, how many, and of which sex. But to the average person these are almost impossible questions to answer. Happily, there are still a few surprises left in life, and procreation is one of them. Although conception can be controlled, it cannot be forced.

So anyone wanting an exact answer to her questions is likely to remain unsatisfied. Even if she visits a palmist. Many practising palmists would find this disappointing statement quite heretical, but we do not believe that children can be predicted with reliable accuracy, so do not want to raise false hopes. Certainly there are lines in the hand which relate directly to children, and on occasion, a prediction can be remarkably precise. But unfortunately not reliably so.

The begetting of children is unquestionably much less rhythmic and natural than it used to be, and so, often lines in the hand can give false hopes or false alarm. In some hands, the skin texture is so fine and soft that Children lines can hardly be seen at all, and are certainly not clear enough to be read. In others, belonging to women who have no children and are well past child-bearing age, healthy children lines may well show up, revealing a possibility that existed, but was never taken up.

People proffering their hands to be read will never be discouraged from asking questions which are difficult to answer, however, and within limits, answers can be attempted, so here we describe the few clues we know to answer the questions you are bound to be asked.

Lines depicting children are found either on the mount, or the finger of Mercury. The lines are vertical and may either run up the mount at right angles to the Marriage lines, or run over the crease between the palm and the little finger, or be seen only on the base of the finger itself. For lines to have a strong meaning they must show up in both hands and be reasonably clearly marked.

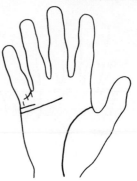

The long lines, approximately one centimetre, signify boys, and the short lines – almost half that length – girls. Only numbers and sequence will be seen, since the lines cannot be put on a time scale. Sequence, by the way, is read from the outside of the palm towards the middle.

If a line is especially deep, much deeper than its peers, brilliance is implied. This child will be very talented and clever, and could well make a name for him or herself.

If a line gives the appearance of being very newly etched (although it could well in fact have been in the hand for a long time) and slightly feathery, the indication is that the woman is pregnant at the time.

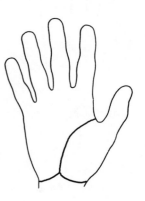

If it appears that no children exist either in the past or in the future (in the hands of women, that is; men very rarely show any Children lines) there is another sign in the hand you can look for to corroborate your theory. If the first bracelet line separating the palm from the wrist bows up towards the centre of the palm, the implication is that the subject will bear no offspring.

TRAVEL LINES

Lines which signify long journeys (to other countries, that is, not just fifty miles to see Aunt Agatha) are found on the outside of the hand, between the wrist and the Heart line, tracing their way a little towards the centre of the palm. As can be expected, people who do a lot of travelling will reveal the most lines . . . although there are other factors to be taken into account, which scramble this simple formula.

Not every journey, for instance, will reveal itself. If it did, an airline pilot would run out of space in a week! Only the important expeditions, which make an impression on the subject's life, etch themselves on the side of the hand.

But real journeys are not the only travels to show. In rare cases you will see a hand with clear Travel lines in evidence, and learn that their holder has never been overseas. However, looking more closely into the hand you will see that such a person has a very clear imagination indicated perhaps by a gently sloping Head line, and could well have travelled extensively, but only in the mind. Very

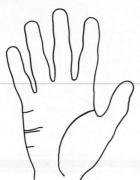

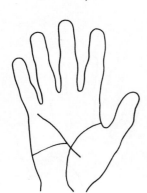

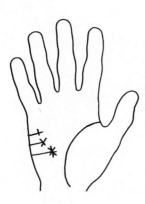

psychic people, too, can sport illusory Travel lines. And in this case, they may have travelled, as a medium, through someone else.

The more powerful a Travel line appears at the time of the reading, the more certain is the journey. And if the most definite line to show up is right in the centre of the palm, the journey is either very recent, or imminent. Travel lines either high up near the Heart line, or low down near the wrist, refer to voyages further removed in time.

A very long Travel line, which marks its way far into the palm of the hand, hitting either the line of Destiny, or the Life line, shows that there is a possibility the subject may emigrate.

If the extended Travel line joins up with one of the clearly marked Affection links coming from the mount of Venus, a relationship with someone abroad could be responsible for the move. The bond is obviously strong, and if this merging of lines bears a branch leading off up towards the mount of Mercury, marriage is the outcome, and emigration almost a certainty.

Often Travel lines join up with the patterns of fine lines in the centre of the hand, and from these patterns, a lot more can be discovered about each individual voyage. However, interpreting the patterns requires not only very advanced skills in palmistry, but also a measure of intuition as well. A little of this exacting art is revealed in the chapter on the Post Graduate Course, enabling you to read more into voyages and travel.

If a Travel line is crossed by a vertical line, some sort of fear accompanies travelling. In general terms this can be a fear of flying, a dislike of the sea, an acute instability which makes foreign places seem to be frightening. However, if the line crosses only one Travel line in particular – the most prominent, most immediate line, perhaps, the fear is of a more specific nature. One particular journey is surrounded by a cloud of doubt.

A cross on a Travel line could well give rise to this doubt, since it often signifies some sort of accident *en route*. Travel lines change frequently, however, and if the cross shows in the right hand only, it could well be possible to avoid making a particular journey when the crossed line is most prominent.

A star terminating a Travel line does not relate to a particular journey and it is unlikely that its implication can be avoided for as long as it lasts. Death by drowning is the traditional meaning of this mark.

There is a line which can be confused with the marrying of Travel and Affection lines – and the confusion would certainly be unfortunate, since the other similar line highlights the susceptibility of the subject to addiction of some sort. To make sure you can distinguish between the two, study the characteristics of the Addiction line, on page 62.

THE GIRDLE OF VENUS

The Girdle of Venus is another elusive line which can by no means be relied upon to show up in every hand. And when you understand its meaning, you will see why, because it relates to an aspect of nature which is certainly not common to everyone.

A perfectly formed Girdle (which, incidentally, is rare) traces its way in a semi-circle beginning between the fingers of Jupiter and Saturn, and ending between the fingers of Mercury and the Sun. The line may however, be less direct, shorter, exist only in part, or be broken up, and the meaning of the mark alters for each different manifestation.

Occasionally, the Girdle of Venus can appear to be part of, or at least connected to, the Heart line, and this association is not merely incidental, since the meanings of each line are indeed connected as well. For the Girdle of Venus reflects sensitivity, great depths of emotional feeling, physical lust and a desire to take feelings and sensations to extremes.

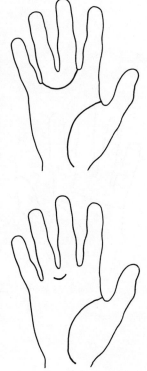

A long and clearly marked Girdle of Venus is held in the hands of people who thrive on excitement and thrills. They feel intensely all the various emotions that are available to us, (including, incidentally, love) and constantly seek yet more excitement and variety. They are liable to experiment in any new medium that will give them a charge: drugs, the excessive use of alcohol, various sexual deviations, and their pursuit of the Ultimate Experience can, in very extreme cases, rule their lives. Looking at the healthier characteristics of this rather excessive mark, those people with a long Girdle of Venus in their hands can also be expected to have a highly developed appreciation of the arts. They will be very receptive and sensitive and also have a warm, lovable side to their nature as well.

A short Girdle of Venus is a much more moderate sign. People who hold just a suggestion of a complete Girdle in their hands will also be sensitive and emotional types, original in outlook and probably sensuously sexy as well. They will be capable of great emotional involvement and depth of feeling, but will not crave to push their fantasies and desires to the limits.

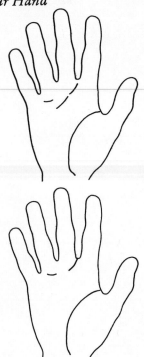

Sometimes you will come across a Girdle that agrees with neither of these descriptions, being long, and yet fragmented, so that the course of the line is far from clear. In this case, a high level of sensitivity exists, but is liable to be misdirected. The holder of this sign will be mercurial, and his or her emotions will swing between extremes of total involvement and indifference; the quest for thrills and the need for calm. Emotionally, these are difficult people to be involved with.

Just a hint of the Girdle of Venus, tracing only a small part of its course, shows that a capacity for consuming emotional feelings exists, but other, more rational forces in the subject's character push this extreme force into perspective. This is a good sign to have, since it shows that although a person is sensitive and highly tuned emotionally, he or she is also likely to be reasonable and adaptable as well.

In addition to the major and minor lines, there are two particular configurations which must be considered along with these lines.

THE QUADRANGLE

The Quadrangle is the name given to the space between the Heart and the Head lines, and from its shape and proportions you can make further judgements about some superficial character traits. This is a useful adjunct to the detailed reading of lines, because even if you are not formally reading a person's hands, and only catch a glimpse of the palm, this simple shape will show up and give away a few secrets.

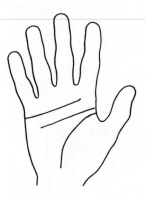

The best Quadrangle to have is about a centimetre wide and regular in shape – the Heart and the Head lines being near to parallel. This denotes an evenness of temper, and a good sense of humour. The symmetry of shape shows that someone is reasonable and broadminded, given neither to wild extravagances, nor to bouts of introversion and depression. Those with such Quadrangles in their hands are likely to have the push necessary to make headway with their lives. If a Psychic Cross (see page 75) is found in the centre of a space of these proportions, it can be seen as the embodiment of clear vision, so long as there are few other lines crowding round to cloud the interpretation.

If the Quadrangle is regular, but narrow, with both the major lines running close together, it is a sign of a character rather lacking in imagination and sense of humour. With the Head and Heart lines running close to each other, feelings of the heart are allowed to cloud the clarity of the mind; the pragmatic mind to sway the strong feelings of the heart. The sum total is a ditherer, someone who cannot single-mindedly pursue any career, or resolutely rush into romance.

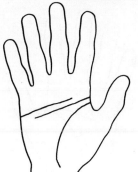

A very wide Quadrangle is an excessive sign held in the hands of people who tend to be gullible. Such people lack a sense of purpose and rely too much on others, being easily led and lacking backbone.

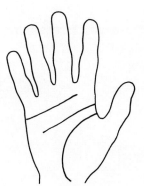

If the Quadrangle is irregular – wider at one end than the other – it shows a tendency towards imbalance. It is found in the hand of people who live their lives to extremes, jubilant one moment and totally dejected the next. If the Quadrangle is narrower under the finger of Jupiter and wider beneath Mercury, the bouts of depression are liable to be more acute.

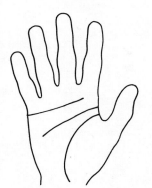

A waisted Quadrangle, wider at both ends than in the middle, usually suggests that the subject will have a rather uncertain, unconfident period in mid-life. This sign often shows itself in the hands of worriers, who naturally have very lined hands.

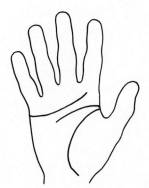

THE GREAT TRIANGLE

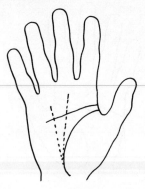

The appearance of the Great Triangle in the hand is a mark of an imminent – or recent – breakthrough, and is always associated with accomplishment and success. The Triangle is made up of the Life line, the Head line, and the more erratic lines of either Destiny, or the Sun. When the various elements of a scheme are about to come together, the third, transient line will be seen to start making its way across the gap. When achievement is definite and absolute, the Triangle will suddenly show up quite prominently, only to fade away again if the glory is only temporary.

7

MINOR MARKS

So far we have discussed the major lines, which do alter, but neither very often, nor very radically, and the prominent minor lines, which are marginally more mobile and flexible. But looking at any but the simplest, cleanest hand, you will see sometimes scores of other less obvious lines and marks which are very fine in quality and changeable in character.

These very fine lines can only be interpreted after a lot of experience has been accrued, using great skill and, in time, intuition. The majority are discussed in Chapter 10, the Post Graduate Course. At this stage, however, there are some marks which are easy to identify, simple to interpret, and which add yet more enlightenment to character and events.

Studying fairly coarse-textured hands with the naked eye, and finer, less obviously marked hands under a magnifying glass, you will see some patterns and shapes that are easy to recognize. Some lines, for instance can be seen to form a complete square or triangle, others a well-defined cross or star. These marks are small and, depending on where they fall in the hand, they each tell a different story.

A **square** may be just that or be the crossing of two pairs of parallel lines. And to have a precise and definable meaning, it must either straddle a line, or lie independently on one of the mounts.

A **triangle,** in this instance, is definitely formed in its own right, and not just the chance product of crossing lines. It can be found on any of the mounts and, rarely, nestling against one of the major lines. Very lined palms may well appear to hold a great number of

69

triangles, but in the centre of the hand, these are seldom independent shapes, and usually lose their significance because they are simply the bi-product of another pattern.

A **cross** has to be free standing to have a meaning. Of course complicated hand patterns will reveal hosts of crosses caused simply by the intersection of lines, and these can usually be overlooked (or at least deferred until the Post Graduate course is tackled). But small crosses either on the mounts, or on one of the principal lines deserve further consideration at this stage.

Stars look a bit like asterisks and, again, are either found on the mounts, or at the termination of the major lines. Sometimes they may be incorporated into a line – the Sun line for example – and in this case highlight the meaning of the line.

An **Island** is formed when a clearly defined line branches out into two before resuming its singular state. It may appear on any line at all, and relates to a specific event which, depending on where the island appears on the line, can roughly be timed. **Chaining,** like a series of attached islands, generally relates to setbacks, either to progress or to health.

Grilles, as the name suggests, are patches of lattice crossing either the mounts, or in rare cases, one of the lines. Grilles are never a good sign, but are almost always topical, and can lift as quickly as they appear.

All these minor marks may be transient. Although we are born with all the principal lines well formed in our hands, finer lines, patterns and marks can develop and disappear all through life. Certain of these outlines described above will remain in the hand for a lifetime, especially those, of course, which relate to a character trait. Others, related to specific events, will be seen to show up at the appropriate time, only to fade away again when the incident or danger is passed. Reading your own hands, you can determine propitious times to embark on new projects when certain signs begin to show in your hands. You can also see periods when it is advisable to be a little more cautious than normal, when certain aspects of your life appear to be under threat.

Squares

Taking squares first, we will look into the meanings of the mark wherever it appears in the hand. In general, squares will be found to act as a repair factor. On a line they can act as a bridge over a difficult period; on a mount, a contradiction to an adverse force.

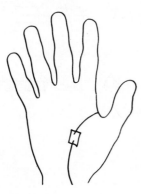

If you see a square on the Life line it is usual for it to surround a flaw of some sort. The flaw quite possibly points to some sort of threat to the constitution – an illness, perhaps, or an accident, but the effects are diminished by the square, which acts as a kind of guarantee. Because of its presence, it can be assumed that either the setback will be of a very minor nature, or will pass unnoticed altogether.

A square on the Head line can again have overtones of a health guarantee. A damaged Head line can indicate either a blow, or an illness affecting the brain, but if you see a square surrounding the defect, its effects will easily be contained. Looking at the hand of someone who suffered from a dangerous attack of meningitis, an island on the Head line is clearly visible, but this is enclosed within a square, showing that the illness was considerably less serious than it could have been.

A kink in the Head line points out a serious error of judgement, but if a well placed square exists, the repercussions will have been, or will be, minimal.

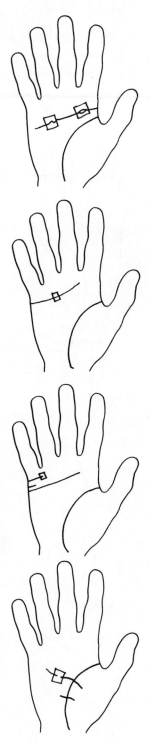

Found on the Heart line, a square points to happiness following a period of rejection and misery. On the right hand, it is a very good sign to have, and promises a period of happiness and emotional satisfaction.

Occasionally, you will find a small square either crossing or terminating the most prominent Marriage line. From the Marriage line itself, it is difficult to assess if the subject is married, or likely to become so in the future. However, once this has been established, you can interpret the meaning of the square. In the hand of an unmarried person, a square on the Marriage line suggests that any hindrances to a happy future as a couple will be ironed out. The existence of the square in the left hand reveals that stumbling blocks may well have presented themselves in the past but that they will not exist for ever. A square on the Marriage line has the same ability to patch up difficulties for married people as well. Even if the relationship has appeared to be irredeemably stormy, the square heralds a period (possibly an indefinite period) of peace and harmony. Shown in the left hand, the tranquillity will already have been felt; in the right hand, it may still be due to arrive.

It is difficult to isolate a square on an Affection line showing up on the mount of Venus, because usually a number of crossing lines exist. However, when an Affection line breaks out of the area enclosed by the Life line, making its way towards the mount and finger of Mercury, it may well be subject to breaks and marks. One

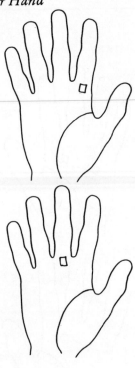

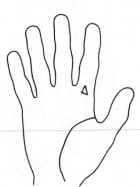

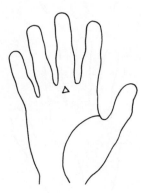

such mark could be the healing square, which indicates a cessation of emotional strife and squabbles.

The square's healing and repair qualities also carry through to the mounts, safeguarding an interest or aspiration in a particular field.

If a square is clearly seen on the mount of Jupiter, it relates to the ambitions. However far away fulfilment of a particular dream may seem, the square ensures that the vision will eventually be realized; not necessarily immediately, but certainly in the end.

The mount and finger of Saturn are always associated with unwelcome influences, and if these influences are highlighted in any way, their power is magnified. The square, however, serves to contain the damage. The most desirable mount of Saturn to have is quite clean, unmarked and not raised. If lines do show up on the mount, it is best that they trace the shape of either a square or a triangle. The square implies the conquering of difficulties, in the past on the left hand, and yet to come on the right.

Triangles

Well formed, independent triangles are welcome signs wherever they fall. They are likely to be quite short-lived, and so their meaning – especially on the major lines – can be assumed to be pertinent at the time of the reading.

A triangle on the mount of Jupiter indicates that the great effort that has been put into work of late is likely to pay off.

On Saturn, a triangle points to special psychic powers, which if well directed, can be a great asset to their holder. However, positioned on this slightly unfortunate mount, the subject should be advised to take care, and not to exploit this unusual gift. A desire to delve too deeply into the occult, for example, could bring rather unexpected and unwelcome results. But treated with caution and respect, this extra intuition will prove to be a bonus rather than a bane.

A triangle positioned on the mount of the Sun points to fairly radical changes, either in lifestyle, or in environment or career, bringing with them unexpected rewards. These changes may not be planned, and if the triangle shows up in the right hand alone, they could come as quite a surprise.

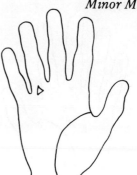

The Mercury mount is customarily associated with business matters, and so it is of little surprise that a triangle positioned here heralds promotion, or the acquisition of new skills.

When attached to any of the major lines, a triangle highlights a happy event. Its timing can very roughly be guessed at – one third along the length of the line corresponding with the late twenties or early thirties; two thirds the mid fifties or sixties, and near the termination point, old age.

On the Life line, the triangle points to general contentment and well being; on the Head line, a cultural or intellectual experience of note; on the Heart line, a fulfilling emotional experience.

Crosses

Crosses are rather unpredictable marks because, depending where they are situated, they may either boast great achievement, or foretell misfortune. Here positioning is all important in the analysis.

A well formed cross on the mount of Jupiter, for instance, denotes an exceptionally happy marriage. This may well show up on the left hand of someone who is not yet married, but in this instance, a contented, fulfilling union can be read as the overriding goal. In the right hand, this much coveted cross points to the most likely possibility – and in both hands together – a fortunate certainty. If the cross is very small, and fairly poorly defined, the meaning is much more superficial, merely indicating the likelihood of a wedding – probably somebody else's wedding – in the near future.

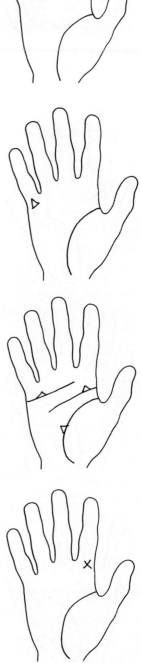

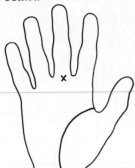

On the mount of Saturn, a cross points to the possible exploitation of the gift of intuition. People holding this sign are likely to dabble in the occult; not out of healthy curiosity, but to try to satisfy their own ends.

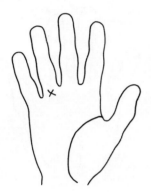

On the mount of the Sun, a small, free-standing cross indicates an unfortunate deal resulting in the loss of considerable sums of money. If the cross is actually made up of a short bar crossing the Sun line, the signs are that ambition and promise will never be fulfilled. Despite a good start, insuperable hindrances prevent the subject from reaching his or her goal.

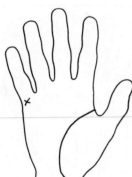

A cross on the mount of Mercury is a fairly unlovable sign, highlighting the existence of deceit. Someone holding this mark either plans, or has just committed, an act of unfaithfulness either to a partner, or to the accepted moral code.

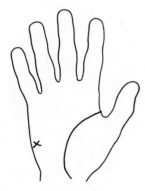

On the mount of the Moon, down on the outside of the hand, a cross signifies a change of environment. Not always a welcome change, however; sometimes the change is forced by a reduction of circumstances.

If a large cross appears in the centre of the hand, between the lines of Head and Heart, in the area called the Quadrangle, it is known as the Psychic Cross. Occasionally the psychic powers will not yet have been discovered, but the cross implies that they are there, just waiting to be aroused. The clearer, more definite and more isolated the cross, the more concentrated the powers.

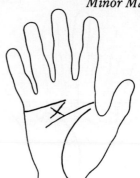

A cross on the Life line unfortunately means an illness. The impact of the malady can be reduced however, if you also see either a square, or a sister Life line backing up the fault.

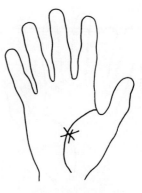

On the Head line, a cross indicates an injury or accident to the head, which may, as with the Life line, be reduced in impact by the existence of a square.

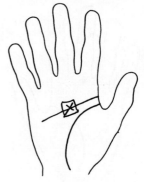

On the Heart line, a cross points either to an emotional trauma, or a strain of a more physical nature.

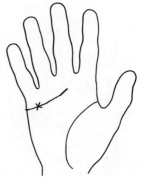

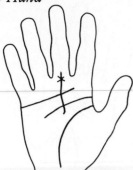

Sited on the line of Destiny, a cross shows that the pre-ordained course of the subject's life has been, or will be, interrupted by someone interfering from outside. Sometimes it is not a person, but an unexpected event or illness that rocks the boat. To cite an example, perhaps a vet develops an allergy to cats, or a pilot fails his medical.

Stars

In general, stars are propitious signs, accentuating the fulfilment of dreams. Here again, there are exceptions, however, where a star may point to a much less desirable circumstance or event. A star, as can be expected, is less common than a simple cross, and so its interpretation is usually rather more extreme.

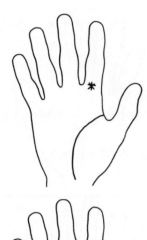

On the mount of Jupiter a star points to consummate happiness derived from total fulfilment. The person holding this sign is certain to have a sunny disposition, and likely to have a genuine love for life. Everything will slot into place – happy marriage, achievement of personal goals, release from money worries – a marvellous sign to have.

A star on the mount of Saturn is a jinx. It brings bad luck to the holder of the sign for as long as it lasts, and is not a good mark to have at all.

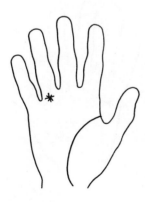

The mount of the Sun is associated with success, and if it is embossed with a star, not only is success likely to be achieved, but it is likely to be accompanied by fame and honour as well. Even within their own lifetimes, people with stars beneath their Sun fingers are unlikely to pass unnoticed in the street. A poorly formed or very tiny star on this particular mount can point to passing notoriety or much more localized, shorter-lived publicity. And the sign, too, will fade quickly from the hand.

Remarkable business achievements usually accompany a star on the mount of Mercury. But, bearing in mind the meaning of a cross on the same mount, these could involve shady practice. A strong line leading from the Head line up to the mount of Mercury is the sign of great flair in the business world, and if this is capped by a star, there should be no doubt about the achievements which will undoubtedly be the result of hard work and good commercial sense.

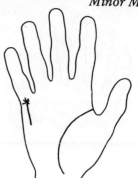

A star positioned between the Head and Heart lines in the Quadrangle should not be confused with the Psychic Cross and its meaning is entirely different. It highlights family friction and power struggles with relatives.

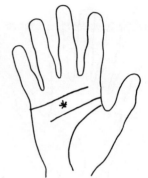

On the mount of Venus, a star indicates that the subject is liable to be deceived or double-crossed by a friend.

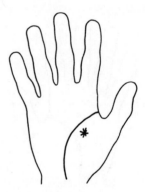

Curiously enough, although the meanings of crosses and stars are sometimes quite different, when positioned on the major lines, their meanings are more or less equivalent. So a star on the Life line points to an illness, and on the Head line, a shock of some sort.

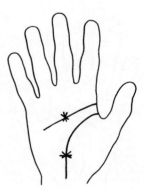

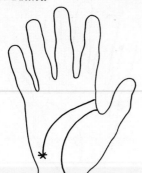

A star at the end of a deeply sloping Head line has a meaning of its own, however, highlighting the depressive nature of someone with this line. In extreme cases, the star can point to a mental illness of some sort.

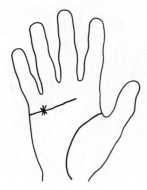

The meaning of a star on the Heart line, too, is different from that of a cross. In this instance, instead of pinpointing an emotional trauma, it suggests a much more welcome event, such as a brief, but exciting affair, which may be either physical, or merely illusory.

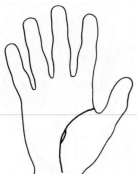

Islands
On whichever line an island appears, it points to a period of weakness, followed by a resumption of strength. On the Life line, an illness is indicated by an island – quite a serious illness if it shows up in the same place on both hands. However the fact that the lines converge back into a single strong line shows that recovery is complete.

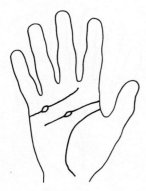

An island on the Head line points to eye strain. And on the Heart line, an island indicates an unfortunate attachment, which brings with it a period of heartache.

Grilles

A grille can crop up almost anywhere in the hand, and where it does, it casts a shadow over the part of the hand in which it appears. Setbacks can be expected, and worrying times usually self-generated, but occasionally caused by factors beyond the subject's control.

A grille on Jupiter signifies very poor judgement, and can sometimes allude to a bad decision, often motivated by vanity or pride. Once taken, the decision could be difficult to reverse, and continues to have an adverse effect for as long as the grille is seen in the hand.

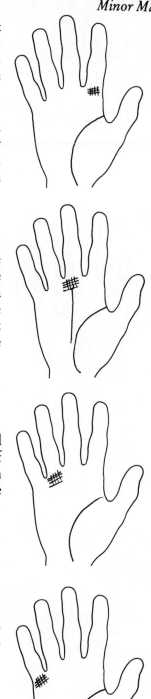

On the mount of Saturn, a grille discloses a period of stagnation, when all drive, ambition and progress are stultified. Seen at the conventional termination point for the line of Destiny, the grille resembles the fragmentation of the subject's fate and future for a period. When this mark is seen in the right hand, it is not advisable to make any changes or long-term plans, because they will almost certainly be thwarted. However, looking on the bright side, the chances are that the sign will soon lift.

The mount of the Sun frequently shows signs of achievement and ambition; when a grille is present, the indications are reversed. If found in the left hand, setbacks will already have been noticed; in the right, they could still be ahead, affecting either the home environment, work or idealistic plans.

A grille on Mercury is more specifically to do with work and with financial transactions, signifying obstacles and disappointment in these areas.

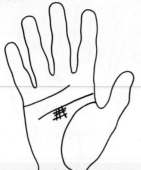

Seen in the centre of the hand, touching on the Quadrangle, a grille highlights outside influences, and unwelcome interference from other people, which may not only warp the subject's judgement, but also weaken resolve and hinder progress in any field.

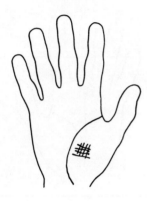

A definite grille on the mount of Venus – not to be confused with a network of Affection lines – shows great lust and a consuming sex urge which may well dominate the direction of the subject's life for a time.

8

PALMISTRY AND PARTNERSHIPS

So far we have looked at the hand as a collection of independent features and the texture, the shape, the proportions have each been closely examined individually. On their own, these draw a clear outline of the character whose hands are being read. If you couple several of the features together, you will find that you can start to colour in certain areas of the picture as well.

Using a very simple mathematical formula (a+b+c=x) it is possible to draw some quite surprising conclusions. Fairly complete character studies can be arrived at, and from these you can see quite clearly the potential compatibility (or incompatibility) of any two people, in close friendships, affairs and marriage. For those who are already 'paired off', the following illumination will not only be fascinating, but also explain some irregularities as well. For those who have still to make the great step into a permanent relationship, on the other hand, hunches and suspicions could be confirmed, inclinations given a more positive foundation, and unfortunate liaisons avoided from the outset.

If you look at people as individual pieces of a jigsaw, it is easy to see how some pieces fit together as though made for each other; others nearly fit, but not quite; and yet more are quite obviously a hopeless match for each other. To fit perfectly, it is necessary for one piece to have a dip to accommodate a corresponding bulge. The facets of the interlocking pieces may be exact opposites, but the fact is that they are entirely compatible.

People are not quite so straightforward and, indeed, similarities are often the strength of many relationships. But the analogy still holds true. Certain types of people, like the pieces of a jigsaw puzzle, are compatible with some types, rub along with others, and definitely clash with a quite different third category.

Of course, most people very easily sort out their soul mates from their potential antagonists themselves. But some characters manage to keep their innermost nature hidden from view, either for the brief period of courtship, or even indefinitely. Here, there is no doubt that palmistry can be a help. Not only do the superficial shape and texture of the hand give insight into character, but also outline some very definite traits (either likeable or dislikeable; compatible or incompatible).

There are as many different 'combinations' of hands as there are people in the world, since every hand is unique. However, some outstanding features will be common to one fairly broadly defined group. We have not attempted to offer full 'identikit' hands to match a particular character type, but have listed together some of the more obvious features you would associate with different personalities. Not all can be expected to appear together in the same hand, but one or two together could highlight areas of potential happiness or difficulty.

In an attempt to classify you, the reader, by type, it is not hand features, but general personality traits that are pinpointed instead. Described below in broad outline are six different feminine and six different masculine characters. Generalizations are infuriating and at first glance you may not wish to align yourself with any of the 'types' described. You may be like one group in some respects and another in others. But there must be one category that suits you more than the rest in the greatest number of respects. You should then be able to look down the check list of features of the hand which will be found in people with whom you are, and with whom you are not, compatible. We hope you find it works!

Brief character sketches of six very different types of women:

1. The very feminine woman who is very conscious of the way she looks. Enjoys the good life, going out and being spoilt. Not a great doer or achiever (although quite capable when it comes down to it). A bit on the lazy side, she would rather delegate (which she does well, having great presence and self confidence), than tackle hard jobs herself.

Signs of compatibility:
An elastic springy palm when held between fingers and thumb, showing that he is vital and enthusiastic and a survivor. He's going to have to be the provider, and a pretty adequate provider if you like your luxuries, so make sure he has a prominent Sun line, as well. A pliable thumb is a good indicator of generosity, and is a good companion to a well-proportioned, uncluttered

Quadrangle, which shows general affability and a good sense of humour. It is essential that your man should be as confident as you are yourself, so look out for that long, strong Jupiter finger, which shows a strong will and a high ego. A Heart line running across the hand to end on the mount of Jupiter is the sign of a loving, kind, sexually well-adjusted chap – he could be a bit of a philanderer, but you can cope with that, and it is probably just what you need to keep you on your toes anyway.

Signs of incompatibility:
Men with oblique-type hands (with all the fingers inclining towards the Sun finger) would definitely not be your type, since they tend to be rather unsure of themselves and would never take the driving test willingly. Not only would you dominate this kind of man, but he would also probably drive you to drink, because he might appear to be so ineffectual. You need a very masculine sort of a man, who would not have a Heart line drooping down towards the Head line at its termination point. A Heart line reaching right the way across the hand and almost curling round the outside underneath the Mercury finger would also be a bad sign in a partner for you, because it shows egocentricity; this man would be far too busy pampering himself to bother about you. You should also steer clear of men with narrow Quadrangles, since their petty-mindedness would, in the end, be bound to get you down.

2. The Mother Earth type, who creates and runs a very comfortable, contented home. Extremely competent at everything she does (give or take the odd detail!), she likes the outdoor life, animals and children and is tolerant and adaptable. She probably has little time for 'frills', and prefers the straightforward pleasures in life to the fine arts; intelligence centres more round common sense than academics.

Signs of compatibility:
The fellow with square hands would probably suit you best, with an evenly matched length of fingers and palm, showing that he is straightforward and down to earth. Nothing much would shake this chap, and he would not be niggly and fussy (which would get on your nerves). His fingers should be fairly pliable, showing a happy-go-lucky outlook to life, and you should also look out for a long Sun finger, which will underline his agreeable nature, showing a love of children and animals. A good, pronounced mount of Venus coupled, perhaps, with a hint of a Girdle of Venus points to a healthy approach to life in physical matters, while a straight, fairly long Head line will show a good brain. If this Head

line bears a branch leading off up towards the mount of Jupiter, you should be especially pleased, since this is the sign of the extrovert, who would fit in very well with your casual pace of life.

Signs of incompatibility:
Of all hand types, the knotty-jointed shape is least likely to be compatible with someone such as yourself. Whereas your life is largely governed by instinct, the man with knotty hands lives entirely through his brain. He is a great thinker, worker, and in many cases, worrier, and he is obsessed with detail. You tend to take a much broader view of life, and a much more physical one (the man with the knots is likely to be rather a chilly lover). Stiff fingers are also a bad sign where you are concerned, since they show an inherent inflexibility, and you are nothing if not easy going. Little will rub you up the wrong way except, perhaps, obstinacy, so give anyone with hard fingerprint cushions a wide berth as well. Your easy nature would find it difficult to cruise along with someone who is either untrustworthy, or who has a bad temper. The most obvious signs of these fairly unlovable traits are a crooked Jupiter finger and a bulbous thumb respectively, so you should avoid these if possible, too.

3. The artistic, idealistic sort, who tends to be vague. A bit of a dreamer, this type tends to leave a lot of issues in her life to chance. Very efficient at what she does – when the mood takes her, that is – but in day to day matters she is a shade impractical. She is not very concerned with outward appearances, and so she and her home may seem a little chaotic.

Signs of compatibility:
Unlike a piece of jigsaw, if you are artistic (and idealistic, by chance), you are unlikely to look for opposite qualities in a mate, and much more inclined to go for a mirror image of yourself. So the man with tapering hands, with pronounced joints and wedge-shaped, splayed fingertips and nails is probably the best bet, since he will be creative and sensitive, and appreciate things of beauty as well as being artistic himself. If his Heart line ends in three branches bursting up towards the fingers, his artistic talents will probably be quite highly developed. A Head line sloping slightly downwards is the best for your opposite number, showing that he is imaginative and has an open mind. If his Sun finger is straight and long, and tends to be favoured more than the Jupiter finger, you will find that he combines kindness with sensitivity, and if he is seriously involved in any branch of the arts, has the foundations for success. Since you tend to be a bit of a dreamer, it would help if your partner were a shade more highly motivated in practical

matters, so look out for a strong line of Destiny and a well etched Sun line to show that he has the drive and ambition to put his talents to good use.

Signs of incompatibility:
Even if you do not go for someone who is as artistically inclined as yourself, your partner would have to have some imagination and vision. This precept would rule out men with square hands and short fingers, since this feature implies a very matter-of-fact disposition. If hands of this type are marked with very few lines, their owner is likely to be rather a basic character who either cannot, or at least does not want to, see beyond his nose, and it is therefore certain that this man would not be for you. A hard palm, when pressed between the fingers and thumb, reveals that its owner is a hard worker and a 'sticker'; this would not in itself be an incompatible characteristic for you, but if the hand were exceptionally hard, feeling almost solid, you could run into problems, since this texture of hand denotes stubbornness and obstinacy. Inflexibility is also shown by a narrow Quadrangle, when the Head line and Heart line are very close, and the roles of each become rather confused. A gently sloping Head line is generally a good sign in a partner for you; however, a line with an exaggerated slope could be less promising, since this shows too highly developed a sensitivity which could lead to instability. Since you could have a tendency to be a little too imaginative, you would certainly need your opposite number to be stable.

4. A very physical person, who is both attracted and attractive to the opposite sex. Likes to have a good time, and can be rather wild at times, and irresponsible. Not very reliable, nor much of a one for routine, but she can be very good-natured, loyal and popular. Despite panache, underneath she is both sensitive and romantic.

Signs of compatibility:
There is no way that you would get on with a mean spirited man. You would want the generous, open type, who is both fun loving and popular (not to say sexy as well). So a very flexible hand is what you should look for, with pliable fingers and thumb and a soft springy palm. The Quadrangle should be wide, and uncluttered in the middle. Both Affection lines and Travel lines are likely to be abundant on such a man's palm, and it would be a good sign for you if there was a small gap between where the Head and Life lines begin, showing that he is the independent type, capable of making up his own mind. The men you get on with are likely to be well-adjusted and active both physically and emotionally; they may well, therefore, have comparatively short fingers, a high mount of

Venus and a long Heart line with numerous fine branches leading off in both directions. Of all people, you would probably best be able to cope with a man with a Simian line (in his left hand preferably) and might even enjoy his unorthodox, unruly nature.

Signs of incompatibility:
Many of the incompatible features of potential partners will show up in their Heart lines – which is possibly not surprising since you hold so much store by the affairs of the heart. A short Heart line, ending on the mount of Saturn, for example, is a bad sign for you, showing that this man is a bit cold, both physically and emotionally, and certainly unromantic. Most long Heart lines are a much healthier sign in a partner for you, with the exception of the line which terminates right up between the fingers of Jupiter and Saturn, since this implies possessiveness and jealousy, which would somewhat cramp your gregarious and flirtatious style. Men with obviously knotty joints to their fingers tend to be the absent-minded-professor types who become bound up in their work, and charming though they may be, they are inclined to neglect their partners emotionally, and sometimes physically as well. This trait could be discordant with your own character, so you would be best advised to avoid not only knotty joints, but anyone with excessively long fingers as well. Stiff fingers, while we are on the subject, are a poor indication for you, too; you need a more flexible fellow with pliable fingers and thumbs, coupled with soft fingerprint pads and springy palms.

5. The career woman who has many interests outside the home. Very active and energetic, she has a good brain and a lively mind. Quite capable herself, but when under pressure, able to delegate as well, she tends to be slightly managing, not least because she runs her life at a quick pace and is impatient when others seem to be too slow. She enjoys play as much as work, but is not very good at relaxing quietly.

Signs of compatibility:
Often successful, highly motivated women feel happiest with men with as much drive and ambition as themselves. Such men could well have square palms with long fingers, showing that they are capable, hard working and reliable (you couldn't be doing with someone who would let you down), and if they hold long, reasonably straight Head lines as well, they will make good headway in their working lives, and operate well in positions of authority. A branch dipping down from the Head line would be a good sign, showing imagination and sensitivity as well (that would keep you on your toes). The best hand texture would be fairly

hard, denoting the ability to work hard and successfully without being assertive or pushy. Such a successful, confident man as we have suggested above, could have a Heart line with two upward sweeping branches towards its termination point. This would be a marvellous sign in a partner for you, denoting not only individual success, but a happy and fulfilling partnership as well. Not all ambitious women want their men to be as go-getting as themselves; some derive reassurance from having a supportive partner whose life depends much less on his own drive. Such a man, the perfect anchor, could well have oblique hands with soft fingerprint pads showing that he is happy to play second fiddle, and would be loving, considerate and loyal in his role.

Signs of incompatibility:
Somebody who is ineffectual and incompetent would be quite wrong for you, so you should avoid if possible those men who carry sure signs in their hands that they are losers. Such signs as a wavy Heart line, for instance, which points to a character who endlessly vacillates, because he doesn't know what he wants; a short thumb, which is a sign of low intellect, and points again to indecisiveness; a short Sun finger which implies muddled thinking and thoughtless impulsiveness. At the opposite end of the character spectrum, anyone who thinks too much of himself, the true egotist, would rub you up the wrong way, and signals of this trait are a Heart line which makes its way right across the palm to the other side (not to be confused with the Simian line, see page 44), and a very long, dominant Jupiter finger, which naturally stands slightly in front of the other fingers, showing super-confidence and leadership. Your perfect partner should be open-minded and flexible, and would not, therefore, have either stiff fingers, or a narrow Quadrangle.

6. The domesticated, perfect housewife type, who definitely likes to play second fiddle to her man. Slightly lacking in confidence, and so likes to follow rather than to lead. At work, the perfect secretary who is very good at putting other people's schemes into effect.

Signs of compatibility:
Your perfect partner, though likely to have a square, hard-textured palm, could well have what is called the mixed hand, with two or three different finger types. The essentials here are that he should be home-loving and dependable, well able to cope himself and to provide for you. The line of Destiny is likely to be quite clearly defined in his hand and, in the best of all possible worlds, the Sun line should look important in the hand as well. Where

home life is concerned, a double Heart line is the ideal, the mark of the spouse who puts his wife and home first, come what may. His Marriage line should stand out quite clearly, and possibly be offset by a cross on the mount of Jupiter endorsing the possibility for a very happy marriage. This man requires a degree of confidence, to carry the pair of you through, and so is likely to have a strong Jupiter finger too.

Signs of incompatibility:
One thing you certainly do not want is someone who hopes to be able to lean on you; you want to do the leaning! Men with oblique hand types therefore are definitely out. You should give an equally wide berth to those whose fingers are too flexible, and capable of bending right back on themselves, as this is a sign of someone with too easy going a nature who, rather than make the running himself, would prefer to sit back and let others take the load. A Head line with an exaggerated slope down towards the wrist shows another form of weakness you could well do without; this time brought about by an over-active imagination and a tendency towards depression. If a man has a Heart line running strongly across his hand to end in the middle of the mount of Jupiter, he could well be a bit of a handful where women are concerned, and if you genuinely lack confidence and need constant reassurance, this could be a bit of a worry to you. Likewise the Simian line. Of all types of women described, you would be least likely to tolerate the unusual qualities held by men with Simian lines (dogmatic independence, following more the rules of the jungle than society).

Brief character sketches of six very different types of men:

1. A very masculine man, definitely 'one of the boys', who likes sport and the outdoor life – sociable, gregarious and popular, with a well developed sense of humour. He also tends to be rather domineering; likes women a lot, but is, it must be said, a bit chauvinistic towards them. The traditional roles suit this man best.

Signs of compatibility:
You really want someone who is going to fit in with *your* plans, rather than having to bother to fit in with hers. So your ideal partner will be adaptable, with pliable fingers and thumbs and a well-spaced Quadrangle, soft hearted and amenable (soft finger-print pads), and fairly dependent, as opposed to domineering shown by either an oblique, or possibly oval hand. You do, however, want her to be able to stand on her own feet, and have enough self-assurance to be able to look after herself while you are

doing whatever you have to do. The kind of girl who has a straight line dividing her fingers from her palm, running more or less parallel to the wrist, will have had things fairly easy in her life. She will not have had to struggle to find her particular niche, and so she will not feel at all competitive, and will more than likely feel quite comfortable in the traditional female role. She could well have her own interests, which might be reflected in a slightly downward-inclining Head line, or a pronounced line of Destiny. And it would help if she were an extrovert, in which case a branch leading from the Head line towards the finger of Jupiter could well show up.

Signs of incompatibility:
You want someone who is easy going and is neither too negative, nor too positive. This rules out women with very hard hands, with little or no give in the palm, since they tend to be very stubborn and anti-social; women with very firm fingertip cushions, since these denote strong will and obstinacy; and with a branch running down from the Head line, since this usually points to an irritable nature, and shows someone who is very hard to please. Your ideal partner should be loyal and true to you, so look out for Heart lines which appear like bottle brushes, since these point to flirtatiousness, and to raised mounts of Venus crossed by scores of Affection lines, since these show that there have been, and probably could still be, plenty of opportunities for other affairs. A sense of humour is important to you, so beware of anyone who holds in their hands very narrow Quadrangles, with the Heart and Head lines running too close together.

2. The man who is well on his way up the business ladder, hard-working, dedicated and successful. Tending to be a shade too independent, his relationships with women suffer as a result. He is not very romantic, but caring and considerate (when he has time). He likes his home to be run like a tight ship.

Signs of compatibility:
If most of your energies are channelled towards your career, it is reassuring to know that everything else is running smoothly as well, behind your back. The 'capable coper' could be your ideal woman, and she would probably have square hands with long fingers (if her fingers are not exactly long, don't worry, square hands with short fingers belong to very good cooks!). She will be a great achiever and organizer, and if her palms are springy, will get by, come what may. To make up for your possible neglect in that quarter, if she has a long Heart line, running directly across to the mount of Jupiter, she will be loving, or passionate even, and will have enough confidence to cope with your success. If this long

Heart line bursts into a fan of three branches at the end, and also has a strong branch heading up towards the Sun finger, you will have found your perfect soul mate, and can look forward not just to a successful emotional and physical union, but also to a marriage of minds.

Signs of incompatibility:
Your ideal partner would not be a person of extremes. She would not, for instance, have fingers and thumbs that were too flexible, capable of bending right back on themselves, since this shows a tendency to be altogether too carefree and easy going, irresponsible and unreliable. And her Head line would not dip too strongly down towards the wrist, since this shows a tendency towards depression and instability. She would have to be quite bright for the partnership to be complete on every plane, and so it would be inappropriate for her to have either a very short Head line, or very small thumbs. Independence would be desirable in a partner for you, so you should watch out for the classic sign of dependence on the family for longer than is necessary; this shows up where the Life and Head lines begin. If the two lines run along as one for perhaps as much as a centimetre, it shows that their owner did not leave the parental nest until really quite late, and is likely to be a dependent sort of character as a result.

3. The archetypal day dreamer, who strolls through life with his head in the clouds. An aesthete – and an artist of some sort, probably – who lives his life according to ideals. A thinker rather than a doer, impractical, rather unreliable, but very sensitive, intuitive and possibly psychic as well.

Signs of compatibility:
There are two different hand types which would be held by suitable partners for you, the spatulate hand and the oval hand. The first, with wedge-shaped finger tips, belongs to very creative, artistic types, who are very sensitive to their surroundings, alert and humanitarian. The second, the most attractive hand shape of all, belongs to hedonists and aesthetes, who really appreciate beautiful things – and sensations – being sensuous as well. Neither of these types would be likely to try to make you conform, both having the unusual quality of appreciating things as they *are*, and not as they could be. A long Sun finger, favoured instead of the finger of Jupiter, again points to appreciation of, and talent for, the arts, as does a Heart line with three distinct branches heading towards the fingers, near its termination point. This last sign is a good sign sexually and emotionally, too, showing self-confidence in these areas which lays the foundations for enduring stability.

Signs of incompatibility:
The most basic hand shape is the square palm with short fingers, showing few but the principal lines. This shows a rather matter-of-fact nature, practical, but without vision, and would definitely not be suitable in a soul mate for you. Either short, or stiff (or worse still, both together) thumbs also point to visionary limitations, denoting the bigot, who is not only set in her ways, but has closed her mind to the acceptance of new ideas as well. To be receptive to new ideas, it doesn't do to be too complacent or self-satisfied, since both these exert their own controls on the brain. Girls with a straight line separating their fingers from their palms, running parallel to the wrist are usually accustomed to leading privileged lives, and could well have lost the knack of asking why. They could also be spoilt, incidentally, which wouldn't really fit in with your scheme of things either. A long Jupiter finger could be a bad sign where you are concerned, too, again showing ego, but this time with overtones of being overbearing and bossy.

4. The home-loving type, who would like nothing better than self sufficiency. He loves children, chaos and animals, but needs comforts to be provided for him as well – and if allowed to be, he could become spoilt. He probably has close links with his own family.

Signs of compatibility:
A very cosy relationship could result from you getting together with someone as homespun as yourself, in which case you should look for the double Heart line, first of all, which is the classic sign of the ideal, warm, loving spouse. Someone bearing this sign is very comfortable and secure, happy in the simple life. A long Sun finger coupled with springy finger tips is another sign of a well-developed nesting instinct, and is associated with a love of children and animals. Square hands are the most practical, and with short or average-length fingers point not just to capability, but to genuine flair for cooking and making the very best of what exists. You do not want your partner to be too matter-of-fact, however, so look for a gently sloping Head line, which reveals a good imagination, and if long, a good brain as well. If this long Head line is coupled with a strong Sun line, success is a possibility – you could even find yourself sitting back doing your own thing with your wife as the motive force and provider.

Signs of incompatibility:
If you are a very adaptable sort of man, who genuinely likes gardening and domesticity, you are liable to be put upon, if you do not watch out. Women with oval hands, very soft palms, and fine skin texture are, it must be admitted, rather lazy and will, if they

can, just sit back and watch others do the work. If you are not very tough, this could be the worst kind of partner for you. Those with oblique hand types are also inclined to lean on you. Being rather dependent, women with this hand shape are certainly not self starters and might rely on you to a greater extent than you had bargained for. A woman with disproportionately long fingers could be too cerebral and not earthy enough for you. Another sign of which you should probably be wary, is a very long Heart line, stretching right the way across the palm, showing egocentricity. In the best of all possible worlds, yours should be a partnership of equals. A woman with very waisted thumbs, with a dominant phalange of Will and very slim phalange of Logic, could be too impulsive and headstrong for you and upset the balance, by insisting on charging ahead, doing everything in double quick time without stopping to think.

5. Likes to think of himself as a bit of a Don Juan. An inveterate womanizer and flirt, he spends a lot of time (and money) having a good time, and would definitely be considered by anyone older than himself as irresponsible. He has a soft heart, however, and certainly fantasizes about settling down – even if he does go the wrong way about achieving his dream.

Signs of compatibility:
Girls with oval-shaped palms and slender, rounded fingers with perfectly shaped nails could have been made for you! Sensitive and sensuous, they give love and sex a very important position in their lives. They know how to have fun, have a good time, and like nothing better than to be indulged. Soft palms and fine textured skin usually go with oval hands, and further endorse the hedonism implied in the shape. Women with this hand type are not ones for ordinary routine and are not the greatest 'stickers' when it comes to work. However, they do have great constancy in another area – love. Although they are quite happy playing the field until Mr Right comes along, when he does, and they fall in love, it is for ever. You could find that you need a slightly tougher character if you are determined to hang on to your freedom forever, in which case you could find your match with a woman bearing a Simian line in one of her hands: she will certainly be independent, and sufficiently unusual to keep you up to the mark. The classic signs of sexuality are a high mount of Venus crossed with plenty of Affection lines, and the Girdle of Venus (by no means present in all hands), so if you really mean business, you should look out for these sure giveaways in the hand.

Signs of incompatibility:
It is impossible, as we all unfortunately know, to devote a hundred per cent of your energy to work and another hundred per cent to having a good time – one has to take priority. For women with square hands with long fingers and good Head lines, the priority is bound to be work; without doubt these are the great achievers among us. Your attentions and suggestions could take second place in the order of things, so you would probably be better off directing your devotion elsewhere. Knotty joints are another bad sign for you to find in a woman's hands, since these belong to women, if not bound up in their work, at least caught up in some consuming philosophy. Potential worriers, such great thinkers might not have time for the frivolities you have in mind. (Incidentally, the Head line dipping down too deeply into the palm is another pointer towards worry.) Another sort of worry you might well have cause to be concerned about is jealousy. A jealous woman would certainly not be entirely suitable as a partner for you, so steer clear of Heart lines running right up to terminate between the fingers of Jupiter and Saturn.

6. No one likes to think of themselves as 'ordinary', but this man leads a pretty conventional, normal life. He works hard and sticks to the daily routine without complaint. Very practical and meticulous, he takes on – and does well – no end of D.I.Y. jobs but enjoys the quiet life, being more of an introvert than an extrovert.

Signs of compatibility:
Whatever hand type you eventually go for, one thing is clear: it should be reasonably free from minor lines, only the principal lines showing up clearly. These should not be too long (except the Life line, of course) and should be very direct, with no exaggerated slopes in either direction. This will show that their owner is an honest, straightforward, uncomplicated woman with few surprises up her sleeve. The Heart line should, for example, make for the mount of Saturn, showing that she is an orderly, regular sort of person who, although a shade cautious, is loving and loyal. The Head line should make its way straight across the hand, showing a good brain which is not governed either by the emotions or the imagination. If the Head line runs with the Life line for a short distance where it begins, this could be a good sign for you, denoting dependence on family, which could easily, if you like, be transformed to dependence on you. The thumb is a good indicator of impulsiveness and willpower; probably neither quality would rate in your list of the top ten credentials of a perfect spouse, so you should look out for the well balanced thumb with equal importance given to each phalange. This indicates good

powers of reason, the sort of person who stops and thinks before she acts.

Signs of incompatibility:

You want a relaxed, appreciative sort of woman in your life, who will not be so extreme as to rock the boat. Highly strung personalities who live off their nerves could conflict with your relaxed scheme of things, so some instant signs that may knock some candidates out of the running right away are nail biting and knuckle cracking, both obvious signs of taut nerves. Someone who is too domineering could try to nudge your routine off the rails, so long, leading Jupiter fingers are definitely out, since these show egocentricity and the desire to lead, to push and to shove. A short Sun finger points to muddled thinking and foolhardiness, qualities you could well do without, while long Mercury fingers could be equally infuriating to you in their way, signalling the inveterate chatterbox.

9
LINKING HANDS WITH CAREERS

Piecing together various pieces of information given by the shape, the texture, the lines of the hand, it is also possible to link a person with a particular type of work. An aptitude for social work, a good head for numbers or the unbiased logic of a lawyer, for instance, may show itself. Not everyone, of course, is in the ideal job, and so palmistry shows only the hidden potentials.

If someone is unhappy at work, the palms could well show up a different area where they would feel more confident and comfortable. If another character seems to be frustrated and unfulfilled, it could be that work takes him or her into the right area, but along the wrong branch. There are many signs of contentment in hands, and these are likely to be prominent when the subject is fortuitously in precisely the right niche.

Since a career forms a large part of most people's lives, it is of course an important part of palm reading as well. Not only is it edifying to pinpoint the aptitudes or vocation of the person whose hands are being read, but useful as well, especially where teenagers are concerned. Looking at the hands of someone who has not yet decided on a particular career it is not only possible to see areas of potential fulfilment, but also to avoid frustration later on.

Here we have divided the spectrum of careers into categories, giving with each the description of a model hand. Where possible, the field has been narrowed down further, connecting specific features in the hand with a precise job. If you want to use this chapter as a kind of 'advice centre', read the hand descriptions first, and see which of these best matches your subject's hand. You will then be able to identify an area – or areas – of natural bent. Taking the job descriptions themselves first, on the other hand, you can then look at the matching hand description to assess suitability.

MEDICINE

Long, straight fingers without any sort of inclination are a feature of the typical medical hand. These have oval tips, and being of significantly different lengths, give the top of the hand an oval appearance as well. The fingers and the thumb are pliable, and the latter is well balanced, with neither the phalange of Will nor of Reason dominating the proportions. The texture of the skin is soft and smooth, and when pressed between the fingers and the thumb, the centre of the palm is firm. The Heart line will seem prominent, being strong and well etched. The Head line slopes very gradually down towards the wrist. The mounts of Venus and the Moon on either side of the hand are raised, indicating benevolence and sympathy.

All **doctors** and senior medics of any kind will, of course, have strong, long Head lines, showing a good brain, and the Quadrangle will be open and generally uncluttered except for the appearance, in a great number of doctors' hands, of the Psychic Cross. The finger of Mercury is frequently pointed, showing tact, and it is interesting to note (and there seems to be no explanation for this) that the half-moons at the base of the nails are usually generous and clear in a doctor's hands.

The Psychic Cross will almost always be present in a **psychologist's** or **psychiatrist's** hands, along with a semi-circle running from below the finger of Mercury towards the centre of the palm and then back to the base of the mount of the Moon. Both these signs point to highly developed powers of intuition. The fingers will be very flexible and the Head line will have a noticeable downward slope.

A **surgeon's** fingers are particularly long, showing capability for minute detail. The skin texture is firm, and the Head line deep and long enough almost to reach to the outside of the palm. Because of the nature of the work, surgeons' hands, incidentally, are always strong.

The hands of a person well suited to **nursing** are similar to a doctor's in most respects. Differences worth noting are that the Head line may well be joined to the Life line above the thumb, and may extend no further than two-thirds of the way across the palm. Looking at the back of the hands, the skin pattern is generally quite distinctive, having the appearance of being coarsely textured. Those particularly suited to working with children will have a long Sun finger and springy fingertips.

Dentists and doctors also share much in common in their

hands, except that the features will be less obvious in a dentist's hands. The fingers are particularly flexible and the texture of the skin noticeably soft.

As an extension of the medical business, it is not surprising that a **vet's** hands should resemble those of a doctor as well. The Sun finger, however, will stand out to be the dominant finger, being straight, strong and long.

SOCIAL WORK

The hands of people such as **charity workers,** or **probation officers**, tend to be on the small side, with spatulate fingers and springy fingertip pads. The Mercury finger is likely to be comparatively slim. Those people who are good at working with others characteristically have firm skin texture and their hands can feel quite hard. The over-all appearance of the palm is that it is very lined, with the Heart line appearing to be particularly deeply etched. The Head line, beginning away from the start of the Life line, is almost straight, with little slope down towards the wrist. The mounts are all raised, particularly the Mount of Venus, which can almost seem to dominate the hand.

THE LAW

Lawyers of all types are distinguished by their square palms – denoting competence and reliability – and long fingers which appear longer than the palm itself. The palm is flat, with insignificant mounts and the fingers lying close together. The thumb is heavy in appearance, the phalange of Reason being well developed. The Heart line is straight, with little inclination up towards the fingers, and frequently forked. The Head line should be straight, with little or no dip down towards the wrist.

The line of Destiny will be prominent in a **solicitor's** hand, coupled with, in the more ambitious types, a good Sun line too. The Quadrangle will be even but not unduly wide.

Of all branches of the law, **barristers** must be the most self-assured and confident. Their Jupiter fingers, therefore, are long and strong. The Head line could well be forked – the branch going straight across the palm showing a good memory; the branch dipping down towards the wrist, a sensitive imagination. There is much to be seen in common with an actor's hands.

A **policeman's** hands are usually regular in shape, either square with square fingers, or a strong oval hand with oval fingers. The hands will be powerful, but with a flexible, sometimes waisted, thumb and a long strong finger of Saturn.

JOBS DEMANDING PRECISION

Large hands with very long fingers characteristically accompany a good head for detail. The fingers will most likely incline, as in the oblique hand, and one of the fingers – not all – could well be bent. At a glance, the fingers seem to be longer than the palm, and are very pliable. The lines on the palm appear to be very deeply etched – particularly the major lines. The Heart line is deep and stretches up to terminate between the fingers of Jupiter and Saturn, while the Head line is equally excessive, making its way almost across to the outer edge of the palm.

Knotty hands, knotty fingers and waisted palms are the hallmark of the **scientist.** The fingers are long, apparently much longer than the palm. The Mercury finger is slim and straight, the thumb well balanced and flexible. The Head line is deeply etched and very long. The mounts of Venus and the Moon will show up prominently.

For a **librarian,** a spatulate hand is the most likely type, or possibly square with long lean fingers. The palm will be firm and the skin texture quite hard. The Head line, long and deeply etched, will start quite high up the palm, well away from the Life line.

People well suited to being **curators** or **archivists** will probably have oval hands, with fairly fine-textured skin. The Head line could well be forked. There is a possibility that the rare double Head line could be seen here too, among a mass of patterns on a very lined hand. The mount of Mercury will be noticeably high.

ENGINEER, MECHANIC

These are characterized by a spatulate hand, with flexible, narrow fingers and thumbs. The skin texture is firm and the centre of the palm springy and pliable, while the fingertip pads are hard. The finger of Mercury is particularly small, and the fingers all lean slightly towards the finger of Jupiter. The palm is broad and the mounts hardly raised at all. The Head and Life lines begin together and run in tandem for a while before branching out on their own. Lines of both Destiny and the Sun are deeply etched.

AGRICULTURE AND HORTICULTURE

Farmers and **gardeners** of all sorts often have square hands with square fingers, the palm and the finger tips hard when squeezed. The thumb will be fairly small with the nail phalange larger than the shaft of the thumb between the two knuckles. The texture of the skin is invariably hard and the palm itself has very shallow mounts, giving the appearance of being almost flat.

COOK

Natural **cooks** have two distinct hand types, either a small, square hand with proportionally small fingers, or a tapering palm with short, oval fingers, whose shape somehow seems discordant with the palm. The texture of the hand is soft, almost flabby, and the fingers are exceptionally flexible. The Head line slopes quite definitely down towards the wrist.

BUSINESSMAN

The hand will have an overall square appearance, with a long, slender palm and long, strong fingers, possibly with knotty knuckles. The line of Destiny shows up strongly in the business person's hand, frequently accompanied by a parallel line denoting business acumen, tracing its way up over the mount of Mercury to the Mercury finger. The Quadrangle between the Heart and Head lines is not too wide – if this gap in the centre of the palm seems too generous, the subject will be too soft and susceptible for the business life.

The texture of a **stockbroker's** hands is soft (though not flabby nor clammy) and the fingers and thumbs are quite stiff. The Sun finger is particularly long, almost as long as the finger of Saturn, a sign of someone prepared to take risks and gambles without faltering or being swayed by the judgement of others. The shape is likely to be square, with long square fingers.

Manager (including **shopkeeper**, etc): Square hands with medium to long square fingers, tending to be stiff, rather than flexible. The palm is quite hard when squeezed. The Mercury finger is slim and straight, the Jupiter finger strong and favoured. The Sun line will show up, and will probably be accompanied by a parallel Business line running over the mount of Mercury. The Head line is likely to start independently from the Life line. The Quadrangle should be regular and average in size, showing the ability to make decisions. The thumb is long and quite heavy.

No matter what shape of hand this person has, the fingers of a **dealer** or **salesman** will seem to be shorter than the palm and may well be slightly inclined or bent – possibly as in the oblique hand. The Business line running up towards the finger of Mercury is prominent and could well spring from the Head line. The Quadrangle could be narrow, possibly with branches connecting the Heart line and the Head line together. If the two run close together, these could in fact be the making of an embryonic Simian line. The thumb will be long, and set quite high in the hand.

An **accountant,** or someone in an allied job concerned with figures, should have square palms which feel quite firm when pressed between thumb and fingers. The skin texture is also fairly hard and the predominantly knotty fingers – probably knotty on both joints – are rigid and inflexible. The thumb, too, shows little give, being straight, reasonably long, and apparently square, the phalange of Reason being at least as powerful as the nail phalange of Will.

Glancing at the hand, the Head line seems the most deeply etched, and is long showing a good memory, and almost straight, with very little inclination down towards the wrist. This line will probably stem from the same source as the Life line, and run together with it for a short stretch. The Quadrangle, between the Head and Heart lines, will be of average width and regular. The Sun line heading up towards the Sun finger will be clear (although possibly short, concentrating on the upper half of the hand), and will be accompanied by a parallel line (sometimes known as the Business line) tracing its way up towards the Mercury finger. The combination of these lines together indicates that a person is shrewd. An unusual feature which is associated with a systematic mind and numerical ability, is the slight leaning of the fingers of Jupiter, the Sun and Mercury towards the finger of Saturn.

To be **self employed,** particular attributes are essential and these can be seen in the hand. For instance, the fingers will not leave the palm in a straight line, but with a slope down towards the finger of Mercury on the outside of the palm. The finger of Mercury will be strong, and could well act as a kind of magnet to the Sun line, which could veer in the direction of this finger. Ambition and a sense of purpose will show up in a strong, resolute line of Destiny.

Not everyone who becomes a **secretary** is dedicated to so doing, so the positive indications of this career are few. However, good signs remain a long, tapering hand with slender fingers. An exceptionally long finger of Mercury, a flexible thumb and soft fingertip pads.

ARTIST

An **artist** will probably have a spatulate hand, with pronounced joints and wedge-shaped fingertips. Of the fingers, the Sun finger will be most favoured and used instead of the Jupiter finger more often than not, and will consequently be long and strong. The skin texture will be soft, the palm of the hand have plenty of give when pressed between fingers and thumb and the fingertip pads will be firm. The Head line has a pronounced slope down towards the wrist, while the Heart line will probably end in a fan of three branches bursting up towards the fingers.

Someone whose artistic talents lean towards **writing** is liable to have a very lined hand, with the major lines deeply etched, and crossed by a multitude of ever-changing minor lines.

If the artistic gift is more for **the stage**, the fingers will be noticeably wide apart when relaxed, and unusually flexible. The mount of Mercury will be obviously high, which shows good powers of imitation, and there will be a definite branch leading up from the Life line to the mount of Jupiter, which denotes the extrovert. A long Head line will show a good memory.

Agent/Publisher: Artistic attributes will be apparent in this hand as well, coupled with smooth skin, very long fingers and pronounced mounts at the top of the palm. The thumb will be straight and inflexible, and the fingers oval at the tips. The hand will be generally uncluttered by minor lines, however there will be a semi-circle tracing its way from the mount of Mercury towards the centre of the palm and back to the outside of the palm at the wrist. The Heart line branches into two where it terminates.

An **art dealer** is likely to have square hands with long, square fingers, almost blunt. The Sun finger will be straight and long, with the finger of Saturn leaning slightly towards it. The Head line will be forked, one branch leaning deeply towards the wrist, the other heading determinedly across to the outside of the hand. The Sun line will be well etched, and parallel to it you will see, just faintly, the Business line. Those successful in the world of advertising will reveal, too, a good line of Destiny.

TEACHER

Because the nature of their work is potentially so varied, it stands to reason that teachers can have almost any type of hand. In common, however, they will have flexible fingers with soft fingertip pads and straight, unbending thumbs. The Sun finger will be observed to be particularly long and strong showing a fondness for children. The Heart line will be straight, with little inclination up towards the finger tips.

BEAUTICIAN/HAIRDRESSER

These will have oval shaped hands, with oval-tipped fingers and regularly shaped nails. The skin texture will be soft, the centre of the palm very elastic, and the fingertip pads soft as well. The mount of the Sun and the mount of the Moon will be well developed. The Head line will slope in a slight curve down towards the wrist.

ATHLETE

Athletes will have spatulate hands, with long, broad fingers, well proportioned, but giving the appearance of being blunt. Really dedicated athletes can hold the Simian line in their hands (the marrying of the Head and Heart lines) or merely have a strong branch connecting these two major lines. The texture on the back of the hand appears to be coarse and, incidentally, can tend to be quite hairy as well.

10

THE POST GRADUATE COURSE

It is possible to read palms by the shape and texture of the hand and the character and quality of the lines, using little imagination, and contributing very little yourself. In the last nine chapters, all the facts of the hands and their simple interpretation have been presented as a straightforward formula. Concentrating solely on this information, palms can be read thoroughly. Just by matching up shapes and lines with their meanings, a fundamental character study will emerge, along with a pretty accurate itinerary of past and future events. But it is possible to get much more from palmistry through a combination of experience and highly developed powers of concentration, which helps to tune more finely the innate sixth sense.

In the centre of every palm, there is a network of very fine lines which we have not yet described. Not only do these lines alter radically from person to person, but they also vary in any given hand from week to week. The novice palm reader can safely ignore these lines and will get much more from studying the obvious features of the hand. However, as time goes on, and palm reading becomes a more natural process, these lines could begin to make a contribution as well.

But to get them to speak, it is no use expecting to be able to follow an instant formula. These lines and patterns are a rule unto themselves, and will only reveal a meaning by guiding the palmist's powers of intuition. At this stage, you could well consider that this is going just a bit too far . . . and straying from our undertaking to make the art of palmistry available to everyone in a simple step-by-step guide.

But rather than branching off the path, it is simply travelling just that little bit further along it. Anyone who enjoys reading hands, and who begins to look at palms (and to study them) more regularly, will start to go through a transition. Gradually readings will cease to follow a rigid formula and will follow their own course instead. When concentrating on a hand, the important features will begin to stand out, the meaning of the lines will begin to link up and become more harmonious and you will instinctively feel when you are getting things right.

The reason for the change is less that you have mastered the meanings (a bit like learning your tables), and more that you have learnt to tune in to the person whose hands are being read. This transition never takes place if palm reading is merely treated as a good party piece. Noise and distractions prevent the forming of a link of any sort, and keep palmistry confined within the basic set of rules.

But if you read hands quietly and privately one to one, gradually a breakthrough will take place and you will feel as though you have moved up on to another plane. The reason for this is that you cease merely to act and react, and begin to ponder much more deeply instead. The same transition accompanies meditation, which slowly opens doors into the remoter parts of the brain. Vision is a word which has been used to describe the effects of formal meditation, and it is equally applicable to serious palmistry.

To assist this 'tuning' process with any subject whose hands you are about to read, it will help to follow a very simple routine before you begin. It is best to have a clear and open mind and to eliminate any personal worries and considerations. To do this, first make sure you are relaxed and sitting comfortably, then close your eyes for a minute or two, and concentrate on a void – or think deeply of a piece of black velvet, if you find that easier.

When you feel calm, and your mind is (temporarily, at least) cleared of clutter, you can start to study your subject's hands. As you work through the usual routine, analysing each feature in turn, make sure that you are as receptive to any impulses as you can be. Continue to keep contact with the hands you are reading, and try not to let your attention wander at all. Conversation is distracting, so you could ask your subject to keep questions until you have finished.

When you have been through all the orthodox lines and patterns, spend a little time concentrating on the finer lines in the centre of the palm. To begin with, no matter how clear your mind, how hard your concentration, you will probably be able to make little of what you see. But do not be discouraged. In time, the lines could well start to form themselves into shapes and patterns that you recognize, and this is when you really begin to use the medium of palmistry to the full.

At first, the patterns you see will appear to be either inexplicable, or totally unrelated to the person whose hands are being read. You might, for example, be able to make out a kind of wigwam shape, or the outline of a kite. Your brain is logically trying to see a shape – any shape – and this is the pattern that presents itself. The pattern is being 'forced' and in fact has no meaning of its own.

However, even this elementary attempt at seeing pictures in the hand will prove a point. Look at the same hand again after a short break, and the shape you saw will seem different. In your search for the precise lines which made up the pattern, another shape may well show itself instead. If you concentrate on the hand for a long time, the lines could well appear actually to move.

As your mind concentrates on each line in turn, moving across the hand, the relative importance of the lines will change, as they move very slightly into and out of focus. The effect is like looking at a living organism under the microscope. When your mind is totally receptive to all impulses, the lines could well appear suddenly to stop moving around, and form themselves into a picture. This picture will tell you something about either the present or the future of the person whose hands are being read.

During the early stages, it is helpful to look and see where the picture appears; and to which lines it relates and connects. If, for instance, you see the shape of a boat near the Travel lines, the subject could be going to make some sort of a voyage; a lover's knot on the Heart line points to a new and highly romantic affair.

It would certainly be very simple for cynics to dismiss any such idea as a load of mumbo jumbo. And indeed, in the hands of really pragmatic people with their feet almost concreted to the ground, you will see very few lines in the centre of the palm, and almost no suitable vehicles for the carrying of messages.

However, there is the possibility of receiving and conveying messages between two intuitive people. If you yourself have signs in your hands that you are (potentially, at least) psychic and your subject shows the important sign of the Psychic Cross, you may well begin to receive messages in the form of pictures in the hand. Clairvoyance has a habit of rubbing off from one person to the other. So if you not only spend time studying people's hands but also, in so doing, come into touch with many, even mildly, psychic people, you will become much more receptive yourself.

You will learn to build up your own reference points. Images which have a definite association in your mind will begin to recur, and will convey to you a message. A bell, for instance, may indicate an imminent marriage; an oblong cheque, considerable financial gain; various buildings may become associated with visits to certain countries. In your own pictorial gazetteer, for instance, stars and stripes could symbolize America; the Eiffel Tower, France; a pagoda shape, the Far East; an elephant's head, Africa. And you may well, of course, see images of places you do not recognize. Tell the person whose hands are being read about the pictures none the less, because they will probably recognize the place when they get there, which is not only fascinating for them, but also very reassuring for you. The nearer the centre of the palm you see the picure, the more imminent is the event.

As the minor lines in the hands alter frequently, it stands to reason that there is wide scope for the message-carrying pictures to alter as well. A belief in palmistry is not, it should be stressed, dedicated to the unswervable force of fate. Some people imagine that because something appears in the hand it is irrevocable, but this is not the case at all.

The situations and events seen in the hands have either happened already (when seen in the left hand) or are likely to lie ahead (when seen in the right). However, as has already been said, the circumstances that lie in the future will only be encountered if the subject continues on the particular course that he or she is following at the time of the reading.

If you become experienced and proficient as a palmist, you will be able to see some isolated events in the future quite clearly. Whereas some may be very pleasant, and so constitute good news, others may not be such welcome spectres on the horizon. Were there to be nothing that could be done about the latter, it would certainly be best to keep the details to yourself. But what is written in the minor lines in the hands should be considered less as a certainty, more as a probability. If you see an impending disaster of some sort in a picture or shape in the hand, it can, if appropriate evasive action is taken, be avoided. Likewise, something good may not come about if the surrounding circumstances are altered too radically.

Instead of continuing to theorize, let us look at a couple of real examples. If, when reading a palm, for instance, you get the impression of a cliff or long drop, and intuition tells you to associate this picture with a fall, you could warn the subject against climbing, or taking risks with heights. If the picture you saw is a genuine message, it will probably transpire that the subject will understand the premonition, knowing, perhaps, that he or she has planned a skiing holiday. Your warning may, on the other hand, mean nothing at all . . . at the moment. But chances are that in the near future the subject will be confronted with a height of some sort, and will remember to take care. Nothing, however improbable, should be ignored. Unless you are entirely cynical about the conveyance of messages through the hands (in which case, why are you reading the post graduate course?) everything you see during a reading should be considered.

II

READING CHILDREN'S HANDS

Right from birth, the principal lines show up quite clearly in children's hands. If you manage to get a glimpse of a baby's palm in the first few days of its life (they do seem to keep their fists clenched with some determination at this stage), you will see the Life line, the Head line and the Heart line, all perfectly formed. As the child begins to grow, these lines will extend as well, but will never be seen to alter much in character. For centuries now, palmists have linked the principal lines in the hand with the most fundamental traits of our personalities. It is commonly acknowledged that we are born with the major part of our character already formed, so if palmistry has any meaning at all, it is obvious that the nature of the basic lines in the hand will start as they mean to go on. And so they do.

But it seems somehow irreverent to start to analyse what sort of person a baby will grow up to be before it has had the chance to become conscious of its own existence in the world. And certainly there are arguments against preconceived ideas of any kind interfering with the bringing up of a child, so reading babies' and children's palms, should, we suggest, be treated rather lightly.

As the child begins to mature and to show the first signs of its innate and developing character, however, it is not only interesting – but in ways helpful – to find out a little more about this budding personality. And the most straightforward way of doing this is by looking at the child's hands.

The easiest way to study the hands of a child, is undoubtedly from a print. Not only is it quite fun messing around with either printing ink or lipstick (both, you will be relieved to hear, washable) and taking prints as we have described on page 9, but using a good photostat machine (if you have access to one) is another entertaining – and clean – way of obtaining very acceptable hand prints as well. Don't forget, however, when working from prints, that the hands are reversed, so it is best to label each one when the prints are first made.

It takes some years for definite hand shapes to reveal themselves. Children's hands are notably podgy, and the extra fat camouflages the precise outline of the palm and the fingers underneath. So apart from the comparative length of the thumbs, for instance, you have to rely exclusively on the lines to give what clues they can into personality and projected events.

As we remarked in Chapter 2, when reading hands you generally take the left hand as representing the qualities you were born with, and the right, what you make of your life. You also, to a certain extent, read the left hands as the past, and the right, the future (unless the subject is left handed, in which case these rules are reversed). Not only is it difficult to tell at an early age whether a child is likely to favour the right hand or the left, you can also safely assume that your subject has very little in the way of a past . . .

So until the hands are completely grown and marked with the full complement of minor and fine lines (say in the early twenties), where events are concerned, both hands should be treated as equals. A sign showing in one hand only will be less certain than an identical line or pattern showing in both. As a child grows up, develops and matures, so his or her character comes into its own and begins to shape events. Any projections you see at an early stage are simply possibilities; only the character traits are fixed and sure.

Some of these may well be directly inherited from the parents, in which case you will see the similarities reflected in the hand. If possible, it is useful to look at prints of the parents' hands alongside those of the child. In this way you can follow similar trends, and isolate the less obvious areas where the child's hands – and character – begin to break new ground.

One of the things parents worry about is their children's potential intelligence and abilities. Looking at the Head line, you can see the former clearly indicated, since intellect is directly linked to the length of the line. The longer the line the brighter the child – and the best direction for straight-forward brain power is more or less straight across, with only a slight downward slope.

A long, straight line reveals a very good memory – so children with this feature in their hands have the potential to do well at school. If they do not seem to live up to expectations, you can assume that something is holding them back: laziness (very soft palms and soft skin texture), lack of confidence (short Jupiter finger), too great a dependence on the family (Head and Life lines running together at the start for a distance), and try to do something about it.

A good imagination and potential artistic flair will show up right from the start again in the Head line. This time, a slight downward inclination is what you look for. Artistic types generally also tend to have long fingers and spatulate finger tips, splaying out like wedges. The spatulate hand may well not reveal itself until later on, but you will certainly be able to judge the length of a child's fingers.

Any lines travelling upwards from the wrist towards the fingers can be a healthy sign in a child, showing drive, potential achievement and success. Sometimes these, the lines of Destiny and the Sun, may not come to light until later on, so if they do show up at an early age, their meaning can be assumed to be magnified.

The Heart line will show how warm and loving a child is, and will also suggest how passionate he or she is likely to become later in life. The yardstick here is again the length; the longer, the more demonstrative. When there is more than one child in a family, jealousy can sometimes crop up. Those children who are most likely to feel possessive about their parents, and therefore more threatened by attention paid to their siblings, will in all probability have long Heart lines stretching up between the fingers of Jupiter and Saturn. Unattractive as jealousy may be in others, it is also very poignant and painful for those who experience it as well. When parents understand that these powerful feelings are innate, they can take steps to teach their children to deal with their strong emotions, and possibly be more tactful and understanding, so that, feeling more secure, the children are able to learn.

No parent will really want to look at the Life line too closely, for fear that it reveals something quite unthinkable. However, anyone who is anxious about the quality of this line in a child should be reassured, because as the palm grows, so the Life line can strengthen and extend.

So much for the principal lines; the only minor lines which will show quite clearly at an early stage and remain unchanged into adulthood are the Marriage lines, found on the outside of the palm, between the beginning of the Heart line and the base of the finger of Mercury. From the position of the strongest line, whether it is close to the Heart line, or further up the hand, it is possible to guess when the subject is likely to get married. The nearer the Heart line, the younger; the nearer the finger of Mercury, the later in life.

Turning to the thumbs, for a moment, these very important digits (where palmistry is concerned) may contribute some additional pointers to character. Long thumbs, stretching up to the first joint of the finger of Jupiter, show a good brain. If the thumbs are quite pliable as well, the child will be adaptable and versatile. If quite stiff (in children's terms; don't forget all their joints are much more pliable than adults'), the parents will probably already have noticed that their child is very self-willed. A powerful unyielding thumb shows a tendency towards obstinacy; not a bad sign in itself, since good strength of character is implied as well, but quite awkward to deal with in a child.

12

THE ORIGINS OF PALMISTRY

When palmistry was first referred to in ancient writings, in *De Historia Animalium* by Aristotle, for example, and several books of the Old Testament, the art was probably already formidably old. Ever since it was discovered that each hand and each fingerprint is unique (there is actually a word for fingerprint in Sanscrit, incidentally), fingerprints have been used for identification and palms, for divination.

All over the world – in China, for instance, 4000 years BC, in India 2000 years BC, in ancient Egypt and in ancient Greece, the lines in the hands have been studied and used to foretell future events and to throw light on physical and mental health. Challengers to the veracity of the practice will be comforted to learn that, even in very early times, before the advent of sophisticated means of communication, the same elementary lines and patterns seem to have been credited with more or less the same meanings, in different parts of the world.

By the time the fifteenth century had arrived, interested and educated parties began to commit to paper complicated treatises on the art. From these you can learn that instead of reading each line individually, palmists had begun to make equations from the various patterns of lines – sometimes, it must be admitted, coming up with some fairly astonishing and far-fetched results.

But there are bound to be some extremists in all practices, however honest and laudable those practices may be at their best. And despite the indulgence of exaggeration, palmistry appears to have enjoyed quite a following at this time, both from scholars, and the new class of wandering gypsies who began to spread through Europe in the fifteenth century.

Then, as now, gypsies were renowned for telling fortunes –
especially for money. Their business became quite lucrative, and
also, inevitably, debased. Not only were gypsies outlawed in this
country, but with them the art of palmistry was put in jeopardy as
well. When he came to the throne, James I, following in the
footsteps of both Henry VIII and his daughter, Mary, persecuted
the gypsies, and with them all who dabbled in palmistry, astrology
and magic. Grouped together, they were described in his Act of
Parliament as 'all who traffic with the Devil'.

The science, however, was not crushed (any more than it was,
incidentally, during the nineteenth and first half of the twentieth
centuries, when the Act was revived). Seriously interested parties
continued their studies, and gradually palmistry, or cheirology,
gained both in credibility and respectability.

In the past, intuition has played a much more important role in
medicine and science than it does today. Certainly, there is an
element of intuition involved in palmistry (not, we must add here,
to be confused with clairvoyance), particularly when the reader
becomes more experienced. And throughout the middle ages, this
intuition was much easier to accept than it is today. People were
less cynical, less sceptical; they did not have to see things on
television to believe them to be true. So long as the palmist
appeared to be knowledgeable and not just a fly-by-night, his
word would be taken seriously. Gypsies, incidentally, did erode
the seriousness of the science to some extent, as proved by a tirade
written by a serious palmist in the mid seventeenth century:

> 'I know full well that thus so profitable a Science, hath rather
> merited the name of old wives fables than a useful science.'

Not only did scholars of cheirology try to shake off the
fairground image of their art imparted by the 'vulgar' gypsies, but
in time there was an even more serious movement towards
marrying serious palmistry with scientific research and medical
fact. The two most important works in the nineteenth century
were both written by Frenchmen: D'Arpentigny and
Desbarrolles. D'Arpentigny went deeply into the different hand
types and their relationship to various character traits, while
Desbarrolles, basing his studies on the examination of hundreds of
hands, looked at the palms as the centre of instinctive life, fed by
vital, life-giving fluid. This fluid, he deemed to influence the
height of the mounts and the pattern of the lines. Far fetched
though his medical reasoning may have been, his explanations
were concise, easy to follow, and often accurate. He believed that
both past and future illnesses could be seen in the hands, along
with in the past and still to come, the impulses creating the changes
in the hands coming from the nervous system.

Desbarrolles also put forward the laudable theory that the apparent future as seen in the hands is not irreversible. If no action is taken to the contrary, what is written will come to pass. But we each have a will of our own, and once put on the right track, do indeed have a chance of avoiding the worst.

Cheiro (assuming this name derived from *kheir* meaning hand, in Greek,) is probably the most famous palmist (so far!) this century, and owed all that he knew to the two scholarly Frenchmen of the nineteenth century. Although he built for himself a widespread reputation – and a small fortune – making some extremely accurate predictions, which received a great deal of publicity, he really did little to further the art – or the science.

Since his death, there has been some serious scientific research into hand analysis. Writing in *Mind Map**, a guide to the outward and visible pointers to personality, Anthony Masters states:

> 'Nowadays, hand analysts, be they psychologists or geneticists, realize the significance of the occult antecedent of their science – chirology. The old method of interpretation that began with astronomical symbolism, went through to a study of symbol-fixated lines and finally to a study of the hand as a whole, had always suffered from a scientific snobbishness about its occult roots. It had also suffered from human failings, ranging from enthusiasts' naivety and ineffectiveness to charlatanism. Only now is it recognized as a partial precursor rather than the subject of scientific disdain. Hand analysis has firstly a medical and psychological diagnostic function, secondly a vocational function and thirdly a self-analytical function . . . It is at present a science in its infancy, but it has already made major discoveries.'

That palmistry is now being taken much more seriously is again underlined by the fact that a chapter on diagnosis from the hands is included in the recent book *Alternative Health Guide*.**

While this heavier, more serious side of palmistry continues, so does the entertaining business simply of reading hands for pleasure. We do not go into the health aspects of the palm here, however, because we do not think that such a potentially morbid subject has a place among character traits and events. *Your Hand* has no shocks lurking round the corner, and it is hoped that most surprises will be pleasant.

Bettina Luxon has kept abreast of the developments in research, of course, but here draws only on her own extensive studies and practical experience in palm reading. Her method certainly draws from history, from the lighter-hearted findings of the past, but is also uniquely embellished by her own remarkable findings as well.

*Anthony Masters, Methuen, London, 1980

**Ruth West and Brian Inglis, Michael Joseph, 1983

13

BETTINA LUXON'S OWN INTRODUCTION TO PALMISTRY

Bettina Luxon was born and brought up in north London and, unusually, became interested in hands – and in fact in palmistry – at a very young age. When given the chance, even as a small child she would sit beside her mother and look at both their hands in comparison. She noticed then that her mother's hands were small and soft and really quite different from her own.

Where other children were occupied with drawing houses, trees and people, Bettina would concentrate on her hands, pencilling around her fingers and palms and then drawing lines copied from other hands she had seen. She was very alert not only to the details of hands, but to gestures as well and when out walking, shopping or even sitting on a bus, she would notice how different people held and used their hands and she secretly made notes, building up a code for hidden signs.

She was so interested in hands that a few years later, her mother bought her a book for her birthday on the subject of palmistry. The book became her most treasured possession and added a new dimension to her absorbing hobby. Up until then, Bettina had used her remarkable gifts of intuition to analyse people's characters. Her mother believed that faces could tell you all that you would ever need to know. Armed with her first key to serious palmistry, Bettina soon realized that you could discern a lot more from hands.

She first started to read friends' hands in an amateurish sort of way when she was about fifteen. And right from the start her predictions were remarkably accurate. Very soon, however, valuable though she found the guidelines in her book, her well-tuned powers of intuition guided her away from strictly following the rules. Through experience she built up a whole new code, and for the first time, stretched the parameters of palmistry wider than had ever been considered before.

Bettina attributes her vision to the sixth sense that is inherent in everyone, but utilized only by those who bother to try. During her earliest readings, some of her forecasts were much more specific, much more personalized than could be expected from the traditional interpretation of lines. In one single house of several flats, she told one boy to be careful with his motorbike, because she could see it associated with some sort of material loss: his saddle box had already been broken into and robbed while she spoke. She told another boy of an impending accident, which would be accompanied by some sort of a remuneration connected with a business: within a month, the boy was a passenger in a mini cab that was involved in an accident. He was slightly hurt, but received generous financial compensation from the cab firm. She told an old lady that she was going to move – an apparent impossibility at the time: within weeks the woman received notification of redevelopment of the block of flats, and was rehoused. And she told a young woman that she was going to have a child: the girl had no idea at the time that she was already pregnant.

Not surprisingly news spread quickly about Bettina's skills and her immediate circle of friends widened to take in acquaintances, and in time friends of acquaintances, all of whom wanted her to look at their hands. In four or five years, she had had enough experience, seen enough completely different personalities and hands, to be able to formalize her own set of rules. She was aware of her own unusual talent, and was determined to take it as far as she could.

In her mid-twenties, she had what can only be described as a 'psychic experience' which confirmed her belief in her gift. Suddenly her powers of intuition became much stronger, and the palms she read really began to come to life. If she completely cleared her mind, and then concentrated very hard during a reading, the lines in the hand seemed to spring out and assume their own order of importance. She became aware instantly of the most revealing feature of a hand, and her readings became even more accurate. She then began to look at the lines on the hand through a magnifying glass. This opened up a whole new area of the palm: the fine, sometimes almost invisible, ever-changing lines in the centre of the hand. When studied with undivided concentration, in complete quiet and tranquillity, these lines would seem to form themselves into a picture, which could then be interpreted by its position in the hand, and its proximity to any of the principal or minor lines.

Having first followed all the steps described here, Bettina would then look at the fine lines, and from them she would draw information about people the subjects would meet, about places they would go to, about an astonishing range of forthcoming events in their lives.

To take an example as illustration, a journalist consulted Bettina not long ago, and having given him an orthodox reading about his character and the important formative events of the past, she turned to the fine lines in the centre of the palm. You are going away at Christmas, to a place abroad that is surrounded by water, she said. There are lots of boats there, and it would appear that they are fishing boats (because she saw what she imagined were rods sticking up out of the boats, pointing towards the sky). You will arrive at this place by boat, she continued, and when you land you will walk up a cobbled path, round a corner, where there will be a very beautiful church facing you. She was interrupted by the journalist who repeatedly protested that he had no intention whatever of going away for Christmas. Undeterred she continued. Past the church, you will come to a market place, she insisted, where there will be people under umbrellas selling things from stalls.

The journalist was far from convinced, and dismissed, too, Bettina's prediction that on returning from this apparently mythical trip, he would find a letter from the U.S.A. which could have an impact on his future. The reading took place in September, and it was not until three weeks after Christmas when the journalist contacted Bettina again.

It transpired that, at the last moment and quite out of the blue, the journalist was invited to Venice for Christmas. Indeed he arrived there from the airport by motor launch, and when he went ashore, everything was just as Bettina had foreseen. He was now back in England, and wondering what to do about a job offer he had received from America, could Bettina advise . . .

And here is another unlikely – but accurate – tale. A woman in her late thirties visited Bettina one day, a total stranger who had heard of the palmist's unusual talents. Again, after the usual introduction, Bettina turned her attention to the detailed lines on the woman's palms, seen under her magnifying glass. You have been divorced, but it is not long before you will marry again, Bettina predicted. You will meet your future husband under a bridge, and he will be very good-looking and smartly turned out.

The woman left, slightly mystified. Every time she walked under a bridge, she smiled to herself, remembering what Bettina had said. A few months later, when she was walking along in the pouring rain, she slipped on some sodden leaves while passing under a bridge. Meeting Prince Charming could not have been further from her mind; she had grazed her leg, hurt her hand, muddied her clothes. She pulled herself to her feet and was just picking up her shopping when a car stopped and a man asked if she was all right. Helping her with her things, he volunteered to drive her wherever she was going. They set off in the car, the woman thought to herself, this can't be *him*, because he is anything *but* well turned out! When they passed a café, he asked her if she would like a cup of tea, because she appeared rather shaken. She accepted, and when they got into the café, he took off his coat, apologizing for looking so scruffy – he had just thrown on an old gardening mac to go out in the rain. Underneath he was immaculate. The woman rang Bettina to tell her the story, and to let her know that she was getting married in a few months.

Not only are lay people astonished by Bettina's uncanny accuracy in her predictions, but other palmists, astrologers and mediums are amazed as well. John Travers, a well known astrologer and medium, made an appointment to have his palms read by her and was so impressed that he was among the first to encourage Bettina to write a book on palmistry.

In this memorable reading, Bettina told the astrologer that he was in for a disappointment over a flat he was hoping to buy. But that this was in fact a blessing, since he would move into a house near the sea instead. This seemed very unlikely at the time, since the flat was stretching resources enough as it was. But the prediction did indeed come true in all respects. The owners of the flat withdrew it from the market and by a stroke of good fortune, John Travers quite unexpectedly acquired a house.

Another astrologer who would have no hesitation at all in testifying to Bettina's unique brilliance in her field, is Russell Grant, the Astrologer Royal, and founder president of the British Astrological Psychic Society, B.A.P.S. He had heard good reports about Bettina from so many different quarters, that he decided to test her out for himself. She gave him a reading, which turned out to be as reliably accurate as ever.

Among a great number of other more personal assessments and predictions, Bettina told him that he would be associated with, and appear, on the television. Once again, Bettina's formula worked like magic, and all the things she had predicted came about. Russell Grant made his personal appreciation official, by making Bettina Luxon the consultant palmist for B.A.P.S.

Inevitably, Bettina has no shortage of people coming to her for readings, and those who cannot see her personally, send her hand prints so that she can give them a reading by post. I believe that part of her success lies in the fact that she genuinely likes people so much. And from her own point of view the most satisfactory readings that she gives are those that help people when they are in trouble. Both men and women come to ask for enlightenment concerning emotional tangles; career people ask for assistance with problems at work; all kinds of people want to know about the future of their finances, whether they are going to move house, go abroad, change partners, alter the direction of their lives . . . Bettina endeavours to give constructive help and hope to anyone who comes to her for guidance, and discourages only those people who want her to go into the details of their health. If someone is at a turning point in his life, not only will circumstances change like a kaleidoscope, but so will the minor lines on the hand as well. So a reading can be repeated as often as once a month, and still continue to throw new light on changing circumstances.

The timing of readings is occasionally too poignant to have occurred merely by accident. Bettina seldom asks to read hands, usually her subjects suggest themselves. Once when she was ill in hospital, she was very surprised when a senior doctor came to her and asked her to look at his hands. She felt that he was rather reflective and sad, but couldn't identify the cause. She told him that he had some sort of an anniversary around that time, and he kept very quiet. You are going abroad, she said, and you will go to a place where there is a magnificent building, very ornate, with mosaics on the floor and the walls. Outside, there is something which resembles a long swimming pool, again lined in mosaic and surrounded by grass. There will be people everywhere. Beyond the building, there is a church with no roof. It does, however, have a beautiful window hewn in the stone, and the sun shines through this window making pictures on the floor.

The doctor was visibly moved, and upset. He told Bettina that his wife had died a year ago; had she still been alive, they were to have gone back to the Taj Mahal for their anniversary that week, where they had been for their honeymoon. His wife had loved the little church she described, and his most lasting memory was of her kneeling to pray where the light came in and hit the floor. He in fact felt that the reading had been very reassuring. He had been taken back again to this special place, described so sympathetically by Bettina, who had never been abroad in her life . . .

INDEX